FORMATTING
YOUR
SCREENPLAY

FORMATTING YOUR SCREENPLAY

RICK REICHMAN

PARAGON HOUSE
New York

First edition, 1992
Published in the United States by

Paragon House
90 Fifth Avenue
New York, N.Y. 10011

Manufactured in the United States of America
10 9 8 7 6 5 4 3 2 1

Library of Congress Cataloging-in-Publication Data

Reichman, Rick
       Formatting your screenplay / Rick Reichman. — 1st ed.
          p.   cm. — (Paragon House writer's series)
       Includes bibliographical references and index.
       ISBN 1-55778-434-5:
       1. Motion picture authorship.   2. Motion picture plays—Technique.
    I. Title. II. Series
    PN1996.R425   1992   91–22733
    808.2'3—dc20   CIP

To Jeanne, without whom this book would still be just an idea.

Contents

CONTENTS

Sample Scripts Used in This Book

Acknowledgments

I would like to thank the following people for their valuable help on this book:

Jean Riley Burnett, for her editing and critique of this book and for her faith and encouragement;

James F. Boyle, Adjunct Professor, Peter Stark Program, University of Southern California, for teaching me how to write filmscripts and showing me the importance of good formatting;

Max Young, Director, Continuing Education and Public Service, Tennessee State University, for giving me the chance to teach my first screenwriting classes and for his support;

Nellie Williams, coordinator, Continuing Education and Public Service, Tennessee State University, for keeping everything in order for my classes at Tennessee State and for putting up with me;

Judith F. House, Director of Continuing Education, Georgetown University, for giving me the opportunity to teach at Georgetown and for supporting my workshops there;

John Douglass, Associate Professor and Director, Graduate Film and Video Program, the American University School of Communication, for recommending that I do a chapter on TV format;

Susan Protter; my agent;

PJ Dempsey, my editor at Paragon House;

ACKNOWLEDGMENTS

Betty Brewton Blackburn and Mr. and Mrs. Brainard Chaney, Florence F. Cameron, Susan Chamberlin, Jim Helm, Frank McEvoy, Allan Moyé, Ralph Nurnberger & Susan Tieger and Wanda Warner for allowing me to use excerpts from their scripts;

All My Students, for teaching me so much about writing filmscripts.

Introduction

"I<small>F</small> the script isn't formatted properly, don't even bother to read it." This is the guideline most studio and agency readers follow.

A reader, or coverage editor, reads and reports on scripts—this task is called coverage—that a studio or agency is considering. A reader will probably be the first professional in Los Angeles to see your script, and his or her opinion of your work will often seal its fate.

Of course, every reader wants to find and recommend a great script. But incorrect formatting suggests that the author does not know how to write even an adequate screenplay. Since readers are paid for each script covered, they will not waste their time on a poorly formatted filmscript.

Script form may seem unimportant—indeed, many popular filmwriting books treat it that way. But in an industry to which, according to a May 25, 1989 article in the *Christian Science Monitor,* approximately one hundred thousand screenplays are submitted a year, how a script looks can determine its fate. While good format alone certainly will not ensure a sale, a script without good format has little likelihood of being seriously considered—or even read at all.

So you recognize the importance of good formatting. Where do you find a book that teaches it? Most screenwriting books allot a few pages to formatting and then advise you to duplicate the format found in "production scripts"—scripts you order from script houses or read in libraries.

Reading production scripts is good advice for the purpose of learning screenwriting. However, to learn correct author's format, you need to study "author's scripts."

How do production scripts and author's scripts differ? Production scripts contain camera angles, scene numbers, directive parentheticals, and various technical information, which help in budgeting and shooting the film. The author's script—what you, the author, write—does not contain those production script details.

An author's script is actually easier to write and to read than a production script. Since I began teaching screenwriting, I have never found a book that teaches author's script format. That is why I have written *Formatting Your Screenplay.*

Formatting Your Screenplay is a step-by-step, easy-to-understand guide for anyone who writes or plans to write screenplays. It teaches only author's script form. And it has been my experience that learning this form is the first, but vital, step toward having your screenplay succeed in Hollywood.

Part One

THE JOY OF TEXT

CHAPTER
1

How to Read a Filmscript

While you are familiar with the way a poem, story, or play appears on the page, you may not have read a filmscript. I have included a scene from a screenplay in this chapter. You may have expected a filmscript to resemble a play, but as you will see, filmscript style is unique.

While you read the following scene, notice how information is placed on the page.

EXT. VENICE BEACH - DAY

The sidewalk hums with sounds of people, radios, skate wheels against concrete, and the ocean. The balmy spring Friday has made everyone unusually relaxed, except for the hawkers who set up for the expected weekend.

DENISE AND JASON

talk along the pathway. They do not walk close together, and often separate around skaters, groups, and animals. They pass a man who wears a winged helmet and a Lone Ranger mask. They grin at each other.

> DENISE
> They were both at Berkeley when
> they got married. When it broke
> up, Mom came down here.

> JASON
> I'm sorry.

> DENISE
> It wouldn't have worked from the
> beginning. Dad was hard-core
> S.D.S., and Mom's a witch.

> JASON
> A witch?

> DENISE
> You know, seances, readings,
> midnight doings with the girls.

Denise's sarcasm isn't lost on Jason, but she changes the subject too quickly for him to react.

> DENISE
> (continuing)
> You?

> JASON
> When Dad got home from the war,
> a buddy talked him into moving
> out here. His buddy moved back;
> we stayed.

> DENISE
> I meant you personally.

JASON

stops to dodge a skateboarder. When they return to strolling, he moves closer to Denise.

JASON AND DENISE

> JASON
> Nothing special.

> DENISE
> I don't believe that.

> JASON
> You know, I'm kind of hungry.

Denise sighs.

> DENISE
> Okay, I'll let you off the hook for now, but next time...

She leaves the sentence unfinished, points up the beach.

> JASON
> Ice cream?

> DENISE
> And some pastries up at the cafe. And look, I didn't mean to give you the wrong impression about my mother.

> JASON
> I didn't get any bad impressions.

> DENISE
> I like my mom, and I even dabble in some occult stuff myself.

She smiles nervously.

> DENISE
> (continuing)
> And Mom still does readings and fortunetellings, even though she pretty much just goes through the motions now.

> JASON
> Maybe I should go to her for a reading. I could use someone to tell my future about now.

(CONTINUED)

5

Denise grins, runs ahead.

> DENISE
> Hoped you'd say that. Come on,
> she's right up the beach.

JASON

slams to a halt, appears frightened.

> JASON
> Oh no. I didn't mean right this
> second. I really can't...

But Denise is either too far away to hear or just pays no attention to him. Caught by indecision, Jason hesitates. Finally, he squints into the distance, nods resignedly, and jogs to Denise.

BEACHWALK AREA - A LITTLE LATER

This part has more permanent booths that can be seen from the walkway. Jason and Denise stand beside a makeshift table. They talk to Beth, who is on the other side.

A sign over the table lists prices for palm readings, tarot, astrology, and crystal ball readings. Over the table is a simple, dark tablecloth, and on the table are the various tools of the trade, including a crystal ball.

JASON, BETH, AND DENISE

Beth has dressed plainly in a peasant dress. A scarf ties back her hair, exposing large gold hoop earrings. Beth holds Jason's hand, palm up. Denise sits on the grass a short distance away.

BETH AND JASON

> BETH
> Have you and Denise been friends
> long?

Jason's slightly embarrassed.

> JASON
> Sort of.

Beth doesn't pursue it. With the index finger of her free hand, she points out the lines as she does her reading.

(CONTINUED)

6

> BETH
> If you have a question about the
> past, present, or future, think it
> to yourself. At the end of the
> reading, I'll answer it for you.

Jason nods. Beth begins.

> BETH
> You have a strong, healthy
> lifeline. No serious health
> problems. You'll probably live to
> be 83 or 84.

> BETH
> (continuing)
> A good mind, and a sense of
> imagination.

> BETH
> (continuing)
> You've had recent trouble with a
> romance.

Jason nods.

> BETH
> (continuing)
> Some problems with your family.

This time Jason doesn't acknowledge, as Beth continues to study his
hand.

> BETH
> (continuing)
> You are athletic, popular,
> sensitive, but there is confusion in
> your life.

> BETH
> (continuing)
> You keep your problems locked
> inside. I see...

She pauses. Her eyes glaze. She lays her hand over Jason's palm and
locks her eyes with his.

                                                      (CONTINUED)

                              BETH
               You are at a crossroads in your
               life, Jason. You have a gift -- an
               extraordinary, God-given ability.
               But you've been ignoring it, or
               worse yet, wasting it.

                              BETH
                          (continuing)
               You must have great courage.
               Danger surrounds you and those
               you love. Your gift can save you.
               But if you misuse it, it can destroy
               you.

Beth breaks her intense gaze and removes her hand. Jason sits,
shaken. His forehead gleams with perspiration.

                              BETH
               Did you have anything you wanted
               to ask... past, present, or future?

                              JASON
               No, uh, that was fine. Thank you.

                              BETH
               You're welcome. I hope I'll see you
               again soon.

Jason nods, rises.

WIDER VIEW

Jason walks away. Denise, perplexed, watches him. She goes to follow
him, but Beth calls her over.

DENISE AND BETH

                              DENISE
               What's going on?

                              BETH
               I just want you to be sure how you
               feel about him.

                              DENISE
               I hardly know him. How am I
               supposed to feel?

                                                              (CONTINUED)

                    BETH
          He's special, but he has some
          tough problems. They could lead to
          a lot of --

                    DENISE
          Heartaches?

                    BETH
          If that were all, I wouldn't have
          bothered to say anything.

Denise bites her lip. Beth touches Denise's shoulder, then tries to
reassure her with a smile.

                    BETH
          He's a nice boy. Just be careful.

Denise turns without reacting to her mother's warning. She runs down
the walkway after Jason.

                                        CUT TO:

What did you note?

You saw headings in all capital letters that begin at the left-hand margin. These are called slug lines. (We will cover them in the next chapter.) There are short, single-spaced paragraphs of description called directions. When a character speaks, his name appears in all Caps, beginning at the center of the page. The character's words are centered on the page, single-spaced beneath the name.

The scene ended with CUT TO: placed to the far right of the page. The word CONTINUED is a header and footer on some pages.

You have now spotted some of the main elements of screenplay format.

I am sure you have additional questions about the scene you just read. What do the words EXT. and INT. mean? Why aren't there any camera angles? What is POV? A character's name shows up once in all caps in the directions, but from then on is written in upper- and lower-case letters. Why? In directions some words are in all caps. Why? These questions—and most of your other questions—should be answered by the end of this book.

To illustrate good formatting, I have also included, at the ends of most chapters, excerpts from some my students' screenplays. Each of these excerpts begins with two or more pages of a student's scene, which have been poorly formatted on purpose. The idea is for you to use those two pages as a worksheet.

You will notice that on each of the script pages there are two numbers. The bottom number is the page number of this book. The number at the top right-hand corner of the page is the page number from the script.

Following each worksheet, the entire scene in correct format is presented. Since this book is about author's format, these scenes are included to give you examples of author's format, as well as a good read. In fact, each of the scripts from which the scenes are taken has either been optioned or won or placed in screenwriting contests.

CHAPTER

2

Slug Lines

Slug lines (hereafter referred to as *slugs*) are those always-capped, single-line entries that look like this:

EXT. RESTAURANT - DAY

In a script, a slug is used to introduce a scene or a shot. Why are they called slug lines? In printer's lingo a slug line is a short identifying title or guideline for a section of a running article in a newspaper or magazine. Essentially, a slug has a similar function in a filmscript.

Scenes and Shots

It is essential to understand the difference between a scene and a shot, because each requires its own slug form. For our purposes, we shall label a *shot* as that part of the script that includes the slug and *all* content until the next slug. Each shot reflects a change of location, time of day, and/or the character(s) being focused on, or a shift in the focal point of a continuing action—for example, a shift from an aerial view to a sideline view of a foot race.

Other teachers and writers may have different definitions for the terms scene and shot. Syd

Field, whom many believe wrote the most influential book on screenplay, calls the above script segment a scene.

For our purposes, a scene is a section of the script (generally three-and-one-half to seven pages) possessing a definitive beginning, middle, and end and centering on a theme and/or action. (Syd Field terms this a sequence.)

A *scene* may consist of one shot. More often it is comprised of a sequence of shots that move the scene toward its conclusion. In "Innocent Bystanders," the six-page section you read is a scene. However, the section that begins with the slug on page 31 of the script JASON, BETH, AND DENISE, to the next slug, BETH AND JASON, also on page 31, is a shot.

Before we continue, let's review.

A *shot* is _____ .

A *scene* is _____ .

Primary and Secondary Slugs

Now for another concept. There are two kinds of slugs: primary and secondary. A *primary slug* introduces a scene, and is nearly always the first slug in the scene. The *primary slug* and everything following it up to the next slug is also a shot. Thus the *primary slug* introduces a shot as well as the scene. A *secondary slug* is the first and only slug that heads a *shot*.

Both kinds of slugs are placed flush with the left-hand margin, fourteen spaces or 1.4 inches from the left edge of the paper, and look like the following:

EXT. WASHINGTON MONUMENT - DAY

CAPITOL STEPS

Primary Slugs

To begin, let's consider how to write the primary slug. A primary slug—such as the first example immediately above—always presents three types of information about the scene that follows.

First, the slug denotes whether the scene begins outdoors or indoors. This is easy. If your scene opens outdoors, this is shown by the abbreviation EXT., for exterior. Therefore the WASHINGTON MONUMENT slug begins _____ .

If a scene takes place indoors, this is indicated by the abbreviation INT., for interior. There is no more to it than that.

The location of the scene is the second piece of information required. Your location follows EXT. OR INT. after two spaces.

If the scene opens EXT., the place could be a FIELD, STREET, SIDEWALK, ROOF, SKY,

POOL, OUTER SPACE, (you fill in a few settings)_____, _____or _____. At this point your slug should read:

EXT. SIDEWALK

In most instances you should not specify in the slug which roof or pool it is. But when it is essential that you identify a particular city, monument, street, or place, then include that designation by using a space-hyphen-space or a front slash.

EXT. YELLOWSTONE PARK

EXT. CAPITOL - WASHINGTON, D.C.

EXT. CAPITOL/WASHINGTON, D.C.

Specific identification is also required when the location alternates between two similar environments. In such cases, it would be clearer, for example, to say:

INT. AMANDA'S APARTMENT

INT. TOM'S APARTMENT

rather than simply APARTMENT. Similarly, you may need to identify a particular room in a specific apartment:

AMANDA'S LIVING ROOM

TOM'S DINING ROOM

But do not go overboard in your description, such as:

INT. AMANDA'S APARTMENT NEARBY THE GRAVE WHERE THE GHOST OF CAMPAIGN PROMISES PAST IS BURIED

Save that extra information for direction. (See chapter 3.)

The third component of a primary slug is time of day. Time of day is separated from location by a dash (actually typed as space, hyphen, space) and should also be short and sweet, but specific or general as needed. It can be DAY, NIGHT, MORNING, NOON, SAME TIME, LATER, A FEW MOMENTS LATER, MIDDAY, MIDNIGHT, TWO O'CLOCK, (now you), _____, or _____.

Keep in mind that except for DAY and NIGHT, which are easy to show, the time of day you include in the slug must be indicated visually or through dialogue within the scene. In the directions, for instance, you could specify a clock hanging on the wall. Or in the dialogue, you might have someone mention the time.

A completed primary slug looks like this:

EXT. HEADQUARTERS - DAY

INT. BALLROOM - NIGHT

EXT. STATUE OF VULCAN - BIRMINGHAM - EARLY MORNING

Use of Historical Time

In addition to the types of information included in all primary slugs, the *first* primary slug in your screenplay includes one more element. That element is historical time. In other words, it is 1856, PALEOLITHIC ERA, SPRING 2146, PRESENT, or WEDNESDAY, AUGUST 28, 1968. The historical time should be enclosed in parenthesis, with the last parenthesis mark flush with the right-hand margin (1.4 inches, or fourteen spaces, from the right edge of the paper).

Do not use the year in which you are writing the script when you mean PRESENT. PRESENT refers to whenever the screenplay will be shot. Remember, your screenplay will be produced several years down the road.

Be aware that whatever historical time you choose, you must show in the directions that follow the primary slug how that time should be indicated on the screen. Your very first primary slug will read:

EXT.   HIGH SCHOOL - NIGHT   (WINTER 1963)

EXT.   CHURCH - MORNING   (PRESENT)

EXT.   STREET - DAY   (2121)

14

Secondary Slugs

Each of the remaining shots that comprise the scene is headed by a *secondary slug. Secondary slugs* contain one or only a few words, designating what the audience will see. As long as the action does not move from outdoors to indoors or the time of day does not change drastically, there is no reason to repeat EXT. or INT. or time of day in the secondary slug.

When you shift from outdoors to indoors or vice-versa, or when you change the time, you should reflect that only in the secondary slug of the shot in which that change occurs. Do not repeat EXT., INT., or time of day in the succeeding slugs unless these factors change again.

So while secondary slugs look mostly like this:

CLOCK

TABLE

FRIEDA

FRIEDA AND ED

SMALL PROTEST GROUP

some end up looking like this:

INT. HALLWAY

RACETRACK - DAY

EXT. PARLIAMENT BUILDING - NIGHT

Remember, so long as a slug introduces a shot in an *ongoing scene,* it is a secondary slug.

One question that is asked from time to time is, "Don't secondary slugs direct the director?" The answer is no.

Secondary slugs serve to keep the audience involved in the film by not letting their collective eye rest too long on one thing. You do vary the visual focus of your screenplay for each shot, and therefore provide a "blueprint" for whom, what, and where to film. However, the script still leaves the director in charge of how to handle the camera.

Another reason for including secondary slugs in your script is that you thereby avoid having a scene with a primary slug and then five or six pages of nothing but direction and dialogue. That type of scene becomes monotonous and is difficult to read. A reader needs to be able to visualize shots from different perspectives. The use of secondary slugs keeps the reader's interest by focusing his attention on the who, what, and where of your scene.

Those of you familiar with scripts will have noticed that I do not use camera angles. You might even wonder where and when camera angles are used. In the author's script, the answers are *nowhere* and *never.* Forget CU (CLOSE UP) and MEDIUM SHOT and any slug with the word ANGLE in it. As a writer, you do not have to worry about how a scene should be shot, only that it will be if written well enough.

The chief reason for not using camera angles is that while secondary slugs do not direct the director, camera angles do. It is presumptuous, and bad politics besides, to demonstrate how brilliant you are with a camera when that type of one-upmanship could doom your script's chances. It is, frankly, much easier, and makes a better looking page, to use simple, straight forward slugs.

A Review of the Rules for Slug Lines

1. Slugs should fit on *only one* line.
2. Whenever you end a shot, whether it is with direction, dialogue, or a cut such as CUT TO:, you should always *triple-space* to the next slug, no matter which type of slug it is. (The only exception is the very first, opening slug, which you double-space to from FADE IN:.)
3. You must *double-space* to whatever follows a slug.
4. Either direction or dialogue must always follow a slug. Never follow a slug with another slug or a cut.
5. Never leave a slug an orphan. That is, never leave the slug with nothing following it as the last item on your page.
6. Never use more than eight slugs on a page.
7. Beware of silly slugs, unless used for a reason. I have seen INT. ALBERT, or INT. CAN. Unless you are doing a film like *Fantastic Voyage* or *Innerspace,* how are you going to show INT. ALBERT, or INT. CAN? I have also seen EXT. TABLE. Easier to show, but if all we see is a table, there is no need, until the next slug, to concern ourselves about where that table is. (For INT. and EXT. see page 14.)
8. Do not number your slugs. (Numbered slugs should appear only in production scripts.)
9. Put all slugs in caps.
10. Do *not* use camera angles.

In part one of the following exercise taken from Flo Cameron's "White Bird," I have inserted several errors in the use of slug lines. Go though these pages and edit them using the guidelines you have just learned. Then in part two compare your corrections with the same scene presented correctly as the author wrote it. An asterisk indicates where corrections have been made.

INT. Living Room - Evening Fall, 1917 - Paris

A large, plush room filled with inviting couches and seats. The decor is feminine, rich—burgundy, rose-pink velvets, velours, and silks. MUSIC from a Victrola wafts through the spacious area like a gentle perfume.

Pauchon stands beside a baby grand piano, regaling Jean and three women with some tale of drunken misbehavior. His tale is rewarded with laughter. Two young French soldiers entertain several young cancan dancers.

Charles sits on a damask rose couch with a beautiful woman.

The large, heavy doors leading into the living room open suddenly. Mata Hari enters, wearing a clingy, low-cut silk dress. The conversations and laughter halt. Mata slips swiftly into the room, gliding, as if on air, to the Victrola.

> MATA
> Danielle, what choice in music!
> Really, you can't be trusted.

A woman near the piano blushes. The men near her titter at her embarrassment. Mata removes the record and replaces it with another. She cranks up the Victrola: TANGO MUSIC.

> MATA
> Who can tango?

Jean, enamored, rushes to her. He bows, she curtsies. Jean leads Mata in a vigorous and graceful tango. The party goers watch, captivated.

Charles walks to the windows and lights a cigarette. He peers out into the night, purposely not watching the spectacle.

The song finishes. Mata pecks Jean on the cheek. Enraptured, he doesn't move. He watches Mata place another love SONG—this time French—on the Victrola. Jean gazes hopefully at Mata. She glides, however, to the couch where Charles now sits alone.

INT. MATA AND CHARLES - Paris, Fall, 1917

Mata joins Charles on the couch. He removes a brandy decanter from a cocktail table and looks at her questioningly. She nods. He pours her a snifter of brandy. They toast each other, then sip their drinks. Mata moves closer to Charles.

(CONTINUED)

> MATA
> Do you like to dance slow and
> close?

> CHARLES
> Slow and close is always nice.

Mata strokes his arm lovingly, longingly.

> MATA
> I'll dance any way you desire.

Charles brushes her off him and stands.

> CHARLES
> Maybe sometime when you're not
> so danced out.

DIFFERENT ANGLE

Charles quickly scans the room and spies Pauchon necking with a
pretty cancan dancer seated on the window seat.

> CHARLES
> Pauchon, my friend, it's time to
> go.

Pauchon looks up, startled, incredulous.

> PAUCHON
> Now?

> CHARLES
> Now.

Pauchon shrugs and holds his hands up as if to say, "What can I do?"
to his young dancer friend. Charles turns to Mata.

> CHARLES
> Thank you for inviting us,
> Mademoiselle. It was kind of you.

He kisses Mata's hand, then heads to the door, Pauchon in tow.

ANGLE ON MATA

stares after Charles, baffled. Could it be that her charms are failing
her?

(CONTINUED)

*INT. LIVING ROOM - PARIS - EVENING   (FALL 1917)

A large, plush room filled with inviting couches and love seats. The decor is feminine, rich -- burgundy, rose and pink velvets, velours, and silks. MUSIC from a Victrola wafts through the spacious area like a gentle perfume.

Pauchon stands beside a baby grand piano, regaling Jean and three women with some tale of drunken misbehavior. His tale is rewarded with laughter. Two young French soldiers entertain several young cancan dancers.

Charles sits on a rose damask couch with a beautiful woman.

The large, heavy doors leading into the living room open suddenly. Mata Hari enters, wearing a clingy, low-cut silk dress. The conversations and laughter halt. Mata slips swiftly into the room, gliding, as if on air, to the Victrola.

                         MATA
               Danielle, what choice in music!
               Really, you can't be trusted.

A woman near the piano blushes. The men near her titter at her embarrassment. Mata removes the record and replaces it with another. She cranks up the Victrola: TANGO MUSIC.

                         MATA
               Who can tango?

Jean, enamored, rushes to her. He bows, she curtsies. Jean leads Mata in a vigorous and graceful tango. The partygoers watch, captivated.

Charles walks to the windows and lights a cigarette. He peers out into the night, purposely not watching the spectacle.

The song finishes. Mata pecks Jean on the cheek. Enraptured, he doesn't move. He watches Mata place another love SONG -- this time French -- on the Victrola. Jean gazes hopefully at Mata. She glides, however, to the couch where Charles now sits alone.

*MATA AND CHARLES

Mata joins Charles on the couch. He removes a brandy decanter from a cocktail table and looks at her questioningly. She nods. He pours her a snifter of brandy. They toast each other, then sip their drinks. Mata moves closer to Charles.

                                              (CONTINUED)

19

                    MATA
          Do you like to dance slow and
          close?

                    CHARLES
          Slow and close is always nice.

Mata strokes his arm lovingly, longingly.

                    MATA
          I'll dance any way you desire.

Charles brushes her off him and stands.

                    CHARLES
          Maybe sometime when you're not
          so danced out.

*WIDER VIEW

Charles quickly scans the room and spies Pauchon necking with a
pretty cancan dancer seated on the window seat.

                    CHARLES
          Pauchon, my friend, it's time to
          go.

Pauchon looks up, startled, incredulous.

                    PAUCHON
          Now?

                    CHARLES
          Now.

Pauchon shrugs and holds his hands up as if to say, "What can I do?"
to his young dancer friend. Charles turns to Mata.

                    CHARLES
          Thank you for inviting us,
          Mademoiselle, it was quite kind
          of you.

He kisses Mata's hand, then heads to the door, Pauchon in tow.

*MATA

stares after Charles, baffled. Could it be that her charms are failing
her?

20

INT. HARRY'S NIGHTCLUB - NIGHT   (A WEEK LATER)

Mata performs her exotic Eastern dance onstage. She is lost
amid a flurry of veils.

Charles and Pauchon, in tuxedos, sit at the back of the room.

                    PAUCHON
          Why don't we sit closer to the
          stage? We come here three times
          and sit in the back.

                    CHARLES
          Hush!

                    PAUCHON
          Let's go backstage and let Mata
          know we're here. She told us to
          stop by.

                    CHARLES
          I don't want her to know I'm here.
          Now quiet.

Pauchon mutters "oh" under his breath as if he understands.

Onstage, Mata finishes her dance and leaves the stage.
Pauchon turns to Charles.

                    PAUCHON
          Why not?

Charles smiles tolerantly at him.

                                        CUT TO:

INT. MATA'S BOUDOIR - NIGHT

Mata and an English officer undress each other amid passionate kisses
and candlelight.

UNSEEN PERSON'S POV - MATA AND THE OFFICER

naked from the waist up, are seen through Mata's second
floor apartment window from across the street. The two move
away from the window. GIGGLES, then impassioned SIGHS, waft
out the window to the street below

EXT. STREET

A man, seen from the rear, stands on the sidewalk. Stray leaves blow down the street on the sultry September night.

The figure, restless, paces before coming to a rest under a street lamp.

It is Charles. As he leans against the lamp, a stray kitten rubs against his legs. He changes position and the cat sits.

A young couple, very much in love, pass by Charles and the cat. The man, a young soldier, nods at Charles, who nods back. Charles looks down at the cat.

> CHARLES
> Is it just you and me who are
> alone tonight?

The kitten meows plaintively in response. Charles picks up and strokes the stray as he looks up at Mata's window.

CHARLES'S POV - THE CANDLELIGHT

in Mata's room is extinguished.

EXT. MATA'S APARTMENT BUILDING - LATER THAT NIGHT

The English officer leaves the building. The doorman, used to Mata's nocturnal dalliances, nods to the officer.

ACROSS THE STREET

The officer turns the corner. Charles starts to cross the street to the hotel but notices the stray following him. Charles picks up the animal and places it back on the sidewalk.

> CHARLES
> Stay. I fly solo from here.

The cat stays as Charles crosses the street.

INT. MATA'S BOUDOIR

Soft pink, gold, and white hues and floral patterns predominate. Mata, in a skimpy floral robe, sits at her white and gold vanity table, removing her lipstick with a makeup sponge.

(CONTINUED)

CONTINUED:

As she removes her false eyelashes, Mata is slowly transformed from an erotic, exotic goddess to a natural beauty.

There is movement in the room. Mata SEES the reflection of Charles in her vanity mirror. Startled, she drops the sponge, turns, and gasps.

MATA'S POV - CHARLES

in uniform, leans cockily against the doorway.

MATA

grabs a towel and tries to cover her face with it.

                         MATA
               You shouldn't see me like this.
               I'm... I'm naked without my
               makeup.

WIDER VIEW

Charles walks over to the vanity and picks up the fallen sponge. He dabs it into the bisque porcelain water basin and squeezes it out. Mata turns away from him.

Charles takes her face in his free hands and turns it toward him. He caresses and dabs at Mata's rouged cheeks until all of the camouflage is gone.

Charles is smitten with her clean, pretty face. Mata tries to look away, but Charles won't let her.

                       CHARLES
               This is how I like you.

Mata stares up, enraptured. Charles leans over. The two kiss passionately as Charles slips Mata's robe off her shoulders. Mata rises, facing him.

With one bold gesture, Charles sweeps the top of the vanity clean of its perfumes, makeup, and other protective coverings. Driven by lust, he hurriedly lifts Mata onto the vanity.

Mata's dancer-strong legs clench Charles's hips as their lingering kisses grow wetter and deeper. Thrusting. Grinding. Penetrating.

                                        (CONTINUED)

23

CONTINUED:

The ballet of entwined bodies can be SEEN on the steamfogged vanity mirror. Mata's and Charles's dance of love reaches its climax.

                                        CUT TO:

EXT. MATA'S HOTEL - DAYBREAK

The same doorman guards the entrance. Charles walks out into the morning sun and crosses the street. The stray gambols over to Charles, happy to see him.

                    CHARLES
          Two friends in one night.

He scoops up the cat and tucks it under his arm.

                                        CUT TO:

CHAPTER
3

Direction

Direction is that part of the script that delineates the action and describes characters, settings, and objects. It is the means by which the writer indicates the visual images he or she wants on the screen. For example:

```
The cue ball slams off two rails, bumps the five ball into the side pocket
and stops behind the eight-ball, putting both balls in a direct line with the
corner pocket.
```

Direction is written in single-spaced prose paragraphs. Like all type in a screenplay, direction is always written in pica type—ten spaces to the inch. The margins for directions are 1.4 horizontal inches, or fourteen spaces, from the left edge of the paper. For the right margin, leave a space of between 1.25 inches to 1 inch from the right edge of the paper. *Never* justify the right margin. No matter what precedes a direction paragraph—a slug, dialogue, or another direction paragraph—always double space to the new direction paragraph.

Direction is written in present tense, which gives the story a feeling of immediacy, as though it were playing on the screen before you. Finally, direction follows the same punctuation and grammar rules—with minor exceptions, to be discussed in a later chapter—as other prose.

Writers Write, They Do Not Direct

A misconception many filmwriters have is that direction calls for the writer to perform the jobs of both writer and director. This misconception may stem from filmwriters having read mostly production scripts, or from the similarity between the words "direction" and "director." However, filmscript direction has nothing to do with the director's job. Directions should never indicate camera angles or camera movement. You recall that while slugs are written to designate focal points for the audience's eye, camera angles are not the writer's province.

As stipulated above, direction delineates the action of the script and describes characters, settings, and significant objects. The largest percentage of direction will relate action. Action, like all direction, should be clearly and succinctly written. A reader must be able to follow events quickly, without having to reread or to guess what is happening.

Use of Direction to Introduce and Describe Characters

You write most of a character's physical description when he or she is *first* introduced. When making that introduction, keep in mind these three important guidelines:

1. Write the character's full name, in all caps.
2. Do not over-describe your character.
3. Have a reason in your story for your character to be on the screen.

For a character introduction, sex, age range, and general appearance are usually all that a writer needs to indicate. Specifics such as long, dark hair and magnetic green eyes should be given only if they will play a significant part in your story. Character description should be general because if there are only one or two actresses or actors who physically fit each role, you have already limited your screenplay's chances of being produced.

When your character first appears, he or she should have a function in the scene, so always have your character doing something and always know why your character is needed at that time and that place. Finally, make sure the paragraphs introducing the character are indispensable to the advancement of your story.

Use of Direction to Depict Settings

Additionally, directions depict settings. As with character description, depictions of settings should not be lengthy or too detailed. Providing a few details that convey the atmosphere of the place is superior to presenting a long list of particulars.

Use Of Direction to Depict Objects

At times you may need to describe an object. In such cases direction may be somewhat more detailed, because you do not focus on a particular object unless it plays or will play a vital part in your scene or story. If your object is important enough to demand its own slug line, such as:

PAINTING

or

PHOTOGRAPH

you will employ more descriptive particulars than you would after a slug designating a person or setting.

Action and Description

One recurring question is, "How much of the direction should be concentrated on action, and how much on description?" Think of direction as a sportscast. Most TV or radio sportscasts employ two announcers. The first announcer is the "play-by-play" person. The second is designated as the "color" broadcaster.

The play-by-play announcer relates the action as it happens. The color announcer adds depth, verve, and emotion by giving the listener or viewer an insight into a star player's personality, telling an anecdote about the team or its members, or relating other aspects about the players, the teams, or the contest itself that help the audience better understand or become more involved in the game.

In a sportscast, the play-by-play person should have a much larger role than the color person. That same balance holds true for a script. Play-by-play, or action, will comprise the larger part of your direction.

Direction vs. Dialogue

Another recurring question is "What proportion of a filmscript should be direction, and what proportion dialogue?" The general rule is that 60 percent or more of a script should be direction, and 40 percent or less dialogue. But 60 percent direction does not mean the writer has a license to loquacity. In direction, economy is essential. Like a good poet, you need to cut excess verbiage and say as much as you need in as few words as possible. A script is only 100 to 120 pages. With so little space, you must choose your words carefully.

Placement of Important Material on the Page

Writing good direction consists, however, of more than selecting the most appropriate phrases and paring away excess. The success of direction also depends on the placement of words on the page.

Readers scan scripts. What they will most likely see is description located close to the horizontal middle of the page. So if your character needs to find a particular computer disk to help solve a case, and you write,

```
BAM. Something smacks him on the head. Just before
he passes out, he sees, by the table, the missing computer disk.
```

the consequential action of finding the disk could easily be missed because it is located at the right margin. But if you place this and all vital information within the page's visual center, it is more likely to be seen:

```
BAM. Something smacks him on the head. Before he
passes out, he sees the missing computer disk.
```

How to Write Effective Direction

Clear writing is one of the most important elements in the success of your screenplay. There are a number of good books on the subject of writing well. The lucid, easily understood prose that you find in good scripts comes from hard work and study. There are no simple solutions, but there are some techniques that you can employ immediately.

One good technique is to use present tense verbs as much as possible. Changing an "ing" verb form such as "he is stalking" to "he stalks" cuts the number of words and, moreover, makes the writing more energetic.

The length of direction paragraphs can also cause potential problems for a screenwriter. One of the great aspects of screenplay format is that it is easy to read. But by writing long, unbroken prose passages, you destroy the advantage the form provides. By adding too much detail or injecting too much information, you turn a screenplay into a novel.

Another good way to write easy-to-read pages is to keep your paragraphs short. How short? For most screenplay directions, limit your paragraphs to four lines or fewer.

How do you keep your paragraphs that short? It is really easier to do than it may seem. Because this is not prose per se, paragraphs can be broken at any logical place. If you simply move from one action to the next, you can change paragraphs there, even though the two separate actions may be part of the same chain of events. Or if you move from a general description to a more specific one, you can break the paragraph at that point.

If your paragraph reads:

```
The underground lab is well lit. There are various
instruments, electronic panels, equipment, and a huge reel-
to-reel computer in the room. On one wall is a long desk at
which two men work. Scattered on the desk are papers,
notebooks, slide rules, drawing compasses, and other
equipment. Across from the men, on top of a platform, is an
empty animal cage.
```

you can easily break it after the second sentence so it appears as two direction paragraphs:

```
The underground lab is well lit. There are various
instruments, electronic panels, equipment, and a huge reel-
to-reel computer and terminals in the room.
```

```
Covering one wall is a long desk at which two men work.
Scattered on the desk are papers, notebooks, slide rules,
drawing compasses, and other equipment. Across from the
men, on top of a platform, is an empty animal cage.
```

By limiting most direction paragraphs to four lines, you create a page pleasant to view and easy to read.

There are additional advantages to observing a four-line paragraph limit. You are forced to write more efficiently. For instance, to change a five-line paragraph to four, you would not only replace "he is shooting" with "he shoots," as discussed above, but might also change the phrase "a painful look on his face" to "a painful expression" or "he looks pained." You've not only shortened the paragraph, but also made your writing stronger.

Limiting yourself to no more than four lines per paragraph encourages you to write more visually (externally), more for the viewers' benefit. Also, this rule helps you to pare your writing down to the essential elements of your screenplay.

But even four-line paragraphs might at times be too long. Suppose you want to write a slam-bam action scene. Whether it is a car chase, a battle, or simply a rollicking action extravaganza, one of the major problems with such scenes is that writers get carried away and describe too much.

Most moviegoers and readers have sat through myriad chases, action scenes, and shootouts. Unless your scene is so incredibly different as to warrant abundant detail, keep the description and specifics general. The progress of the action should be charted clearly, with only enough description to involve the reader's emotions and not bog him or her down with particulars that a crew will determine when shooting begins. With action shots, the minimalist approach works best.

But, you think, suppose I have a two-minute action scene, and I keep it to a minimum—say, less than a page. Doesn't that violate the page-a-minute rule? Yes. But there is a style that can help. It is what I term the one-line-one-paragraph style.

Instead of keeping your paragraphs to four lines or fewer, make each paragraph one and only one line. This format changes both the look of the page and the pacing of the shot(s). It helps you keep your screenplay at a page a minute, and enhances its look. And one of the greatest advantages of this format is that it is simple to write, but adds an entirely new dimension to your work. Suppose your action shot reads:

CHASE

Fed's car speeds ahead of his pursuers. He two-wheels a
corner. From an intersection just ahead, two cars emerge
and turn toward Fed. Fed spins his car around, now
facing the pursuing cars.

Fed speeds toward the pursuing cars. At the last second,
he jumps his car onto the sidewalk, around the pursuers. He
guns the car.

STREET SIGN

DEAD END

BEACH FRONT

Fed's car skids sideways onto the beach and stops. The
wheels spin deep into the sand. The pursuing cars halt
nearby, and two men rush Fed's car.

As you can see, the chase takes up fourteen lines, or approximately 3.5 inches, on the page. Suppose, though, you make every line a separate paragraph. Now it reads:

CHASE

Fed's car speeds ahead of the pursuing cars.

Fed two-wheels a corner.

From the intersection just ahead, two cars turn toward Fed.

Fed spins his car around.

He now faces the cars that have been chasing him.

Fed speeds directly at his pursuers.

At the last instant, Fed jumps his car onto the sidewalk.

He zooms around the approaching cars.

```
STREET SIGN

DEAD END


BEACH FRONT

Fed's car skids sideways and stops on the beach.

His wheels spin, digging deep into the sand.

The pursuing cars halt nearby.

Two men rush Fed's car.
```

The same action takes sixteen lines, or approximately 5.5 inches on the page. It also adds a look that is exciting, seems to make the scene move quicker, and is easier to read. By adding inches you add time, which gives a better representation of the screen time you want your shot or scene to take.

Always remember, it is "Lights, Camera, *Action*," not "Lights, Camera, Dialogue." Beginning writers, and some experienced ones, hurt themselves by writing too much yack and not enough act. And that is one of the prime reasons their screenplays get rejected.

A REVIEW OF THE RULES FOR DIRECTION

1. Margins for direction are 1.4 inches, or fourteen spaces, from both the left and right edges of the paper.
2. Direction is written in present tense.
3. Direction is single-spaced within the paragraph.
4. No matter what precedes a direction paragraph—a slug, another direction paragraph, or dialogue—always double-space to the new direction paragraph.
5. With only minor exceptions (discussed in a later chapter), direction follows the same punctuation and grammar rules as all prose.
6. Do not use direction to describe camera movement or camera angles. Never show camera movement or angles in a screenplay.

In part one of the following exercise, taken from Wanda Warner's "Chief to Chief," I have inserted several errors in the use of direction. Go through these pages and edit them using the guidelines you have just learned. Then in part two compare your corrections with the same scene presented correctly as the author wrote it. An asterisk indicates where corrections have been made.

                              TRAVIS
                    Maria, call an ambulance. Manji,
                    get Calvin.

Travis scoops up Racine.

BEDROOM

Camera follows Namruyu as he carries Racine to his bedroom and lays
her on the bed.

As seen from an ANGLE ABOVE THE BED, Namruyu bends down beside
her and takes her hand.

                              NAMRUYU
                    (Do not slip away from me,
                    Racine. You listen to Namruyu. Do
                    not slip away from me.)

Namruyu looked at Travis, his eyes told him he's losing her.

                              NAMRUYU
                    Let me be alone with her.

Travis had shut the door behind him.

HALLWAY

Calvin and Manji run toward the camera. Travis shakes his head and
waves them away.

                              TRAVIS
                    Chief wants you to wait at the
                    door for the ambulance.

Calvin and Manji turn away. A siren blares in the distance.
Travis leans against the hallway wall. His eyes look up to the pictures
of Emily hanging opposite him. He fights back the tears.

                              TRAVIS
                    You look after Racine for the
                    Chief.

32

BEDROOM

Namruyu leans across Racine's lifeless body, grieving. He wipes away tears and engages in a peculiar ritual where the flat palms of his hands move in small, horizontal circles above her head, then down the rest of her body, close but never touching her. All the while he murmurs a song in Malingese.

HALLWAY

Travis gazes at the photograph of Emily.

> CALVIN (O.S.)
> Come this way. Quickly!

An ambulance crew, led by Calvin, rushes past Travis toward the bedroom.

EXT. PATIO - LATER

Travis and Namruyu sit motionlessly in the rockers.

In the b.g., ambulance lights swirl through the darkness. A deputy leans against a sheriff's vehicle talking MOS with Calvin, who smokes a cigarette.

The coroner approaches Namruyu.

> CORONER
> I'm real sorry. I think it was an
> aneurysm. We'll know for sure
> after the autopsy.

> CORONER
> (continuing)
> We'll take her now, Travis. Do the
> autopsy first thing in the morning.

> TRAVIS
> I can't let you do that, Hollis.
> Racine needs to stay here, just for
> tonight.

> CORONER
> What do you mean? You know the
> procedures I have to follow.

> TRAVIS
> I know, but the Chief has his
> procedures, too.

(CONTINUED)

CONTINUED:

> TRAVIS
> Maria, call an ambulance. Manji,
> get Calvin.

Travis scoops up Racine.

BEDROOM

* With Namruyu following, he carries Racine to his bedroom and lays her on the bed.

* Namruyu bends down beside her and takes her hand.

> NAMRUYU
> (Do not slip away from me,
> Racine. You listen to Namruyu. Do
> not slip away from me.)

Namruyu looks at Travis, his eyes * telling him he's losing her.

> NAMRUYU
> Let me be alone with her.

* Travis shuts the door behind him.

HALLWAY

* Calvin and Manji run down the hallway toward Travis. Travis shakes his head and waves them away.

> TRAVIS
> Chief wants you to wait at the
> door for the ambulance.

Calvin and Manji turn away. A * SIREN blares in the distance.

*Travis leans against the hallway wall. His eyes look up to the pictures of Emily hanging opposite him. He fights back the tears.

> TRAVIS
> You look after Racine for the
> Chief.

34

BEDROOM

* Namruyu leans across Racine's lifeless body, grieving.

* He wipes away tears and engages in a peculiar ritual where the flat palms of his hands move in small, horizontal circles above her head, then down the rest of her body, close but never touching her.

All the while he murmurs a song in Malingese.

HALLWAY

* Travis gazes at the photograph of Emily.

                    CALVIN (O.S.)
          Come this way. Quickly!

* An ambulance crew led by Calvin rushes past Travis toward the bedroom.

EXT. PATIO - LATER

Travis and Namruyu sit motionlessly in the rockers.

In the b.g., ambulance lights swirl through the darkness. A deputy leans against a sheriff's vehicle talking MOS with Calvin, who smokes a cigarette.

* The CORONER approaches Namruyu.

                    CORONER
          I'm real sorry. I think it was an
          aneurysm. We'll know for sure
          after the autopsy.

                    CORONER
                    (continuing)
          We'll take her now, Travis. Do the
          autopsy first thing in the morning.

                    TRAVIS
          I can't let you do that, Hollis.
          Racine needs to stay here, just for
          tonight.

                    CORONER
          What do you mean? You know the
          procedures I have to follow.

                              (CONTINUED)

35

                              TRAVIS
                    I know, but the Chief has his
                    procedures, too.

The coroner motions for Travis to follow him onto the lawn, out of
Namruyu's earshot.

LAWN

                              CORONER
                    What if she died from some exotic
                    parasite or... or something
                    contagious?

                              TRAVIS
                    You know better'n that!

                              CORONER
                    She came here from *Africa*, for
                    Pete's sake.

                              TRAVIS
                    Racine was thoroughly examined
                    the minute she got off the plane in
                    Atlanta... Hollis, I'd consider this a
                    favor.

The coroner hesitates, then hollers to an assistant.

                              CORONER
                    You boys need to move the body.
                    I'll come show you.

                              TRAVIS
                    Coffee'll be waiting for you in the
                    morning.

The coroner nods and walks off toward his crew and the deputies.

PATIO

Travis returns to his seat next to Namruyu.

WIDER VIEW

They watch as Racine's body is moved across the lawn to Namruyu's
cottage. Then the various officials climb into their respective vehicles.

                                                        (CONTINUED)

The START of their motors fills the quiet night. As the vehicles turn around, their headlights illuminate Namruyu and Travis sitting quietly in the dark.

The ambulance is the first to leave. Namruyu and Travis watch taillights disappear down the driveway.

In the darkness, Namruyu finally speaks.

                         NAMRUYU
              Thank you, Travis.

                         TRAVIS
              I'll send everyone to bed.

Both men rise. Namruyu heads for the cottage.

LAWN

Travis wanders over to Maria, Calvin, and other ranchhands huddled on the lawn.

Travis mooches a pack of cigarettes from Calvin. He speaks MOS to the group, which then breaks up. Travis hurries to the machinery barn.

INT. MACHINERY BARN

Travis surveys the engine of a tractor. He is about to unbolt something when he notices the tractor's carburetor and other engine parts laying on the floor.

He pours gasoline over a fistful of rags and briskly wipes the carburetor with the rags.

EXT. COTTAGE

As Travis approaches the cottage carrying the rags and carburetor, Namruyu and Manji exit its front door.

Namruyu takes the items from Travis. He is about to re-enter the cottage when Travis whistles after him and throws him the cigarettes.

MARIA

tiptoes from the main house, toward the cottage.

EXT. COTTAGE

Namruyu exits the house again and joins Travis and Manji on the
lawn.

In moments, flames are visible through the bedroom window. When he
sees this, Travis turns and walks toward the main house.

As he crosses the lawn, Maria steps from a shadow and walks with
him.

As the fire HISSES and ROARS, they look back at the cottage.

COTTAGE

The flames have spread to the roof and gradually engulf the house.
The erect figures of Namruyu and Manji are outlined against the
inferno.

TRAVIS AND MARIA

                    MARIA
          Did Racine reach her God in time?

                    TRAVIS
          Hours to spare.

                    MARIA
          Won't the coroner be suspicious?

                    TRAVIS
          He'll think Chief was stupid to
          clean a carburetor in his bedroom,
          but he'd never dream I'd torch a
          house to burn up a dead woman
          who died of natural causes.

NAMRUYU AND MANJI

drop to the ground, bow their heads in reverence.

                    TRAVIS (O.S.)
          Better tell Calvin tomorrow to
          order some lumber. A carburetor,
          too.

                                        (CONTINUED)

38

CHAPTER
4

Special Slugs

Because slugs indicate what the audience views—how the shot will be seen through the audience's eye—most slugs specify one or more items from your script. These include place, character, object, and time of day. However, there are some generic slugs that a writer may use from time to time to indicate specific types of shots. These slugs—what I term *special slugs*—are SERIES OF SHOTS, MONTAGE, BACK TO SCENE, WIDER VIEW, SPFX, SFX, POV, SPLIT SCREEN, INTERCUTTING, and INT./EXT. Let's define and discuss each separately.

SERIES OF SHOTS

The most used of all the special slugs is SERIES OF SHOTS. Suppose you want to show in abbreviated form a typical day in the life of a writer. You might write:

SERIES OF SHOTS

The following shows a typical day in life of a writer.

A) The writer finishes breakfast, then enters his study.

B) Sunlight streams through the study windows. The clock shows nine o'clock. On the computer screen are the words "Boy meets girl."

C) The clock reads two o'clock. The writer stares at the screen, which still shows only the words "Boy meets girl."

D) Dark of night is seen through the windows. The writer sleeps over the keyboard. The clock says 11:30. The screen reads "Girl meets boy."

A SERIES OF SHOTS is much like a scene in that it is centered on a theme and/or action and has a beginning, middle, and end. But a SERIES OF SHOTS differs in that it is a group of short shots that move a character quickly through a period of time. As in the example above, the slug SERIES OF SHOTS is usually followed by directions explaining briefly what will be shown. Then the actual shots are described in outline form, a double space between each paragraph. Usually there is no dialogue.

MONTAGE

A MONTAGE, often confused with a series of shots, includes two or more images that blend into and out of each other in order to create a particular emotional effect. A montage need not be about a particular character nor be a step-by-step recreation of events. It need not even possess story structure. Dreams, nightmares, hallucinations, and photographs provide some of the most common subjects for the montage. After the slug,

MONTAGE

you could follow either with the outline form:

A) Several video slides of a wedding dance blend.

B) The Washington Redskins tear through the slides.

C) Ice cream and rainbow sprinkles fall gently from the sky.

or with a brief prose or poetic description of the images you want on the screen.

WIDER VIEW

Another slug occasionally used is WIDER VIEW. Admittedly, some might consider this to be a camera angle. However, it does not tell a director how to shoot or where to place the camera, it simply enlarges the area initially seen around a person or object. Many times WIDER VIEW can be used for a visual joke or twist. For instance:

40

HARVEY

sits on the blanket outdoors, talks to an unseen person.

> HARVEY
> Yes, I love you, yes I want you but
> I don't know if...

WIDER VIEW

Harvey talks at a half pint of ice cream.

BACK TO SCENE

BACK TO SCENE is another useful slug. Suppose your scene begins in a large arena such as a barroom:

INT. BARROOM - NIGHT

The fight has gotten out of hand. Kitten, the bouncer, picks up Hal and hurls him across the floor.

if you describe a particular area or incident, such as...

BAR

Hal lands near a young lady. He tips his hat to her, grins, and swings around just in time to K.O. an attacker.

To show to the entire barroom again, you may use...

BACK TO SCENE

SPFX AND SFX

SPFX stands for special effects. A character's dream, Lincoln's ghost haunting the White House, a car exploding, or smoke pouring forth from a building should be labeled SPFX. SPFX is always part of a larger slug, and is written:

EXT. LINCOLN MEMORIAL - NIGHT SPFX

Abe's statue rises from its chair, stretches, and yawns.

SFX is sound effects. SFX involves technical simulation usually done by a special crew. Do not confuse sound effects with music. Sound effects can be the roar of a jet overhead, a distant explosion, or things that go bump in the night. While SPFX and SFX can appear in slugs or directions, they are capped and abbreviated in both:

EXT. CAMPUS - DAY

SFX the ROAR of the jet overhead drowns out the conversation.

or

INT. HALLWAY - NIGHT SFX

From inside armor, something goes BUMP in the knight.

A warning about SPFX and SFX. Don't abuse them. Use them when the effect is something different from what the reader/viewer expects. If Abe's statue moves numerous times, if overhead jet noise is normal, then the effects do not need continuous labeling.

POV

The abbreviation POV stands for point of view. The term is always abbreviated in caps—sometimes written with a period after each letter (P.O.V.). POV is occasionally found in direction but most often in the slug. POV indicates that the audience sees through the eyes of *one* character, usually by means of a straight-ahead shot, without peripheral vision.

It is written:

ROY'S POV

POV is usually followed by a paragraph or two of direction describing what Roy sees and perhaps a sentence or two of dialogue. POV must always be from an organic entity. A car or hockey puck may have a POV only if you anthropomorphize them, as in "My brother the hockey puck." Also, a POV must be from one and only one character at a time.

How do you exit a POV shot? You may use BACK TO SCENE (discussed above) or the name of the person or anthropomorphic being to whom you just assigned a POV.

SPOT'S POV

Some lunatic, dressed in robes and following a floating dagger, yells "Out damn Spot."

SPOT

A third POV exit is to write a slug that moves the reader/viewer to a new setting:

DUNGEON

Spot hears the CREAK of the hallway door and scurries up the stairs.

SPOT'S POV

Some lunatic, etc.

CASTLE HALLWAY

INTERCUTTING

When you INTERCUT, you move rapidly back and forth between two or more locations. The idea is that the actions are happening more or less at the same time. It is good to let the reader know that you are intercutting so he or she can follow the action without becoming confused.

To intercut, write:

DETECTIVE'S OFFICE/CRIMINAL'S HIDEOUT INTERCUTTING

You may also indicate intercutting in direction:

GEORGE AND MARTHA

The following scene intercuts between George in the House and Martha in the Senate.

Or if you intercut among three or more places, you can use:

INTERCUTTING

as the slug, and use directions to describe the people and places in your intercuts.

SPLIT SCREEN

Showing events and people in different locations simultaneously on screen is a situation easily handled by the special slug SPLIT SCREEN. If SPLIT SCREEN is written as a slug, the accompanying direction might explain the subject matter and number of splits the writer intends:

SPLIT SCREEN

Ten shots of simultaneous alien landings on Earth.

Or you might include the subject matter in the slug:

TEN ALIEN LANDINGS SPLIT SCREEN

All landings are shown simultaneously on the screen.

EXT./INT.

The final special slug, EXT./INT. or INT./EXT., is used when you need to show two adjoining sets simultaneously:

INT./EXT. DOORWAY - DAY

Sara, inside her house, speaks with the mysterious stranger on the porch.

The most important consideration in writing all slugs is to make sure you have communicated your intentions clearly. If you decide to do something complicated, do not simply assume that a reader will understand it as easily as you do.

Use the directions that follow special slugs to tell a reader what he or she will read next. Yes, you want a reader involved in the story as if he or she were engaged in a page-turner novel. But you never want someone to wonder what is happening. Give a reader reason to stop, and most likely he or she will. Be clear and correct in slug usage, and you will be closer to writing a good, producable script.

In part one of the following exercise, taken from Allan Moyé's "Hunter's Moon," I have inserted several errors in the use of special slugs. Go through these pages and edit them using the guidelines you have just learned. Then in part two compare your corrections with the same scene presented correctly as the author wrote it. An asterisk indicates where corrections have been made.

EXT. FOREST - SUNDOWN POV

The rain beats down hard and steady as Rachel treks through the
woods. She brushes against a bush of thorns and stops to examine her
leg.

She proceeds through the woods unsure of her direction, switching her
path on occasion. She comes to a small stream and walks down its
bank.

NEARBY TREE spx

Lightning strikes, and the sop of a giant tree explodes, sending
a branch hurtling down to the ground in front of Rachel.
She jumps back, shivering.

RACHEL

puts the case on the ground and sits on top of it, surrendering to her
exhaustion. Her tears are accentuated by various lightning strikes.

HAND

reaches out and touches her on the shoulder. She turns quickly,
frightened.

PETER/RACHEL INTERCUTTING

stands behind Rachel in her robe. He is drenched. The rain and
river are loud. He points upriver.

RACHEL

turns in that direction.

RACHEL'S pov

There is a small waterfall ahead.

PETER AND RACHEL - SPLIT SCREEN

Peter picks up the instrument case and grabs Rachel's arm, leading
her upstream. They step over fallen branches and climb up the bank
toward the falls.

46

EXT./INT. CAVE

They step out of the rain and underneath the falls into a small cave in the rocks.

SERIES OF SHOTS

Peter drops the case to the ground, and flops down against the rocks. Rachel grabs the case, then scoots as far away from him as the small area will allow.

Rachel notices her soaked shirt has become see-through. She turns her back to Peter and tries to wring her shirttails dry.

She gives up and modestly takes the shirt off and replaces it with a sweater from her backpack.

She turns and notices Peter with his knees to his chest, shivering. She has to talk loudly to be heard.

                    RACHEL
          How did you know about this
          cave?

Peter answers facetiously.

                    PETER
          God is my co-pilot.

Rachel unrolls her sleeping bag. As she unzips it, Peter tries to ignore her. She slides closer to him and puts it around his shoulders.

                    RACHEL
          Take off that wet robe. You'll
          catch your death.

Peter looks at her and succumbs. He hands her the wet robe from beneath the bag. She walks toward the falls and wrings it out, letting the water drip down the rocks. Thunder CRACKLES. Rachel jumps back.

                    RACHEL
          Doesn't look like it's going to let
          up.

                    PETER
          So you're also a meteorologist.

                    RACHEL
          If we're going to be stuck here for
          a while, we might at least try to
          get along.

                                        (CONTINUED)

                              PETER
                  How about a prayer meeting?

She pulls the sleeping bag around her bare feet.

Rachel rolls up her pants leg to examine the wound from the thorns.
She finds a small scratch, licks her finger and rubs the wound
repeatedly.

Peter examines the cave and finds a few sticks lying around its
perimeter. He gathers them and brings them to the center of the cave.

After assembling a small pile of wood, he grabs two sticks and
vigorously rubs them together in his palms.

Rachel takes off her boots and rubs her feet in obvious discomfort.

                              RACHEL
                  I think the water shrank these
                  boots.

                                                    (CONTINUED)

EXT. FOREST - SUNDOWN*

The rain beats down hard and steady as Rachel treks through the woods. She brushes against a bush of thorns and stops to examine her leg.

She proceeds through the woods unsure of her direction, switching her path on occasion. She comes to a small stream and walks down its bank.

NEARBY TREE *SPFX

Lightning strikes, and the sop of a giant tree explodes, sending a branch hurtling down to the ground in front of Rachel. She jumps back, shivering.

RACHEL

puts the case on the ground and sits on top of it, surrendering to her exhaustion. Her tears are accentuated by various lightning strikes.

HAND

reaches out and touches her on the shoulder. She turns quickly, frightened.

PETER

stands behind Rachel in her robe. He is drenched. The rain and river are loud. He points upriver.

RACHEL

turns in that direction.

RACHEL'S *POV

There is a small waterfall ahead.

PETER AND RACHEL*

Peter picks up the instrument case and grabs Rachel's arm, leading her upstream. They step over fallen branches and climb up the bank toward the falls.

They step out of the rain and underneath the falls into a small cave in the rocks.

*INT. CAVE

*Peter drops the case to the ground, and flops down against the rocks. Rachel grabs the case, then scoots as far away from him as the small area will allow.

Rachel notices her soaked shirt has become see-through. She turns her back to Peter and tries to wring her shirttails dry.

She gives up and modestly takes the shirt off and replaces it with a sweater from her backpack.

She turns and notices Peter with his knees to his chest, shivering. She has to talk loudly to be heard.

                    RACHEL
          How did you know about this
          cave?

Peter answers facetiously.

                    PETER
          God is my co-pilot.

Rachel unrolls her sleeping bag. As she unzips it, Peter tries to ignore her. She slides closer to him and puts it around his shoulders.

                    RACHEL
          Take off that wet robe. You'll
          catch your death.

Peter looks at her and succumbs. He hands her the wet robe from beneath the bag. She walks toward the falls and wrings it out, letting the water drip down the rocks. Thunder CRACKLES. Rachel jumps back.

                    RACHEL
          Doesn't look like it's going to
          let up.

                    PETER
          So you're also a meteorologist.

                              (CONTINUED)

50

                    RACHEL
          If we're going to be stuck here for
          a while, we might at least try to
          get along.

                    PETER
          How about a prayer meeting?

She pulls the sleeping bag around her bare feet.

Rachel rolls up her pants leg to examine the wound from the
thorns. She finds a small scratch, licks her finger and rubs the
wound repeatedly.

Peter examines the cave and finds a few sticks lying around its
perimeter. He gathers them and brings them to the center of the cave.

After assembling a small pile of wood, he grabs two sticks and
vigorously rubs them together in his palms.

Rachel takes off her boots and rubs her feet in obvious discomfort.

                    RACHEL
          I think the water shrank these
          boots.

She looks at Peter in doubt.

                    RACHEL
          Don't tell me. Boy Scout?

                    PETER
          Life-rank. Twenty-six merit
          badges.

                    RACHEL
          That's comforting.

Peter struggles with the twigs. Finally, he grabs a couple of small
rocks and bangs them together, trying to produce a spark.

Rachel snickers.

Peter sits back, disgusted.

                    PETER
          Everything is too wet. What's in
          the case?

Rachel protectively guards the case.

                                        (CONTINUED)

                    RACHEL
          No way. You're not going to burn
          my cello.

She moves toward the fire.

                    RACHEL
          Let me give it a try.

                    PETER
          Okay, Miss Christina
          Meteorologist.

Rachel pulls herself close to the pile. She waves her arms, magician-
like, over the sticks. Then she slows her histrionics and dips her hand
into her sweater pocket, producing a pack of matches.

                    PETER
          Very funny!

                                        CUT TO:

CHAPTER
5
Dialogue

In filmscript, *dialogue* shows what is said, and by whom. Always written down the horizontal middle of the page, dialogue has three distinct parts: the *character cue*, the *speech*, and the infrequently used *parenthetical*, also known as personal direction.

Character Cues

Begin dialogue with the *character cue*—or speaker's name—in caps and do not underline or center it. Start the character cue at 4.1 inches, forty-one spaces, from the left edge of the paper:

CHARACTER CUE

Begin the character's speech on the line beneath the cue and continue to single-space throughout the speech. If there is not enough space on a page for the character speech to follow the cue, move the cue to the next page. Never leave the character cue as the last item on a page.

Since the speech must read down the center of the page, set your left margin at 2.8 inches, or twenty-eight spaces, from the left edge of the paper and your right margin at 5.6 to 5.8 inches, fifty-six or fifty-eight spaces, from the left edge:

<pre>
                        CHARACTER CUE
              This is where you put the speech
              so it reads down the middle of the
              page.
</pre>

Always double-space from a speech to a new character cue, which begins new dialogue. In fact, no matter what precedes it, always double-space before beginning new dialogue.

Parentheticals

The *parenthetical,* a.k.a. personal direction, refers to instructions to the actors enclosed in parenthesis and placed directly beneath the character cue or sometimes within the speech. When the parenthetical appears directly under the character cue, place the first parenthesis at 3.5 inches, or thirty-five spaces, from the left edge of the paper.

<pre>
                        CHARACTER CUE
                        (parenthetical)
              Dialogue is located here and has
              the margins specified above.
</pre>

The parenthetical may also appear anywhere within the speech.

With one exception, the best way to handle parentheticals is *not to use them at all.* In parentheticals such as:

<pre>
                          JOHN
              (trying to contain his anger)
              I never authorized such a move.
</pre>

the writer is encroaching on the director's and actor's jobs.

There *are* situations in which writers feel that they need to instruct the actors. One instance is when the tone of a character speech may not be obvious from the context, such as with sarcasm. Another is when the speech is directed to a particular person in a group. In such instances, you should put those instructions in direction rather than using the parenthetical:

John contains his anger.

<pre>
                          JOHN
              I never authorized such a move.
</pre>

or:

Cisco eyes the men, then speaks directly to George.

CISCO
This time, we get it right.

The instance in which you *should* use the parenthetical is when an interrupted speaker continues with the same thought or completes a speech after an interruption. When that happens, use the parenthetical "(continuing)."

ROBERT
As Groucho said about love and
money--

JANE
Not that joke again.

ROBERT
(continuing)
love goes out the door when money
comes innuendo.

JANE
If I hear that joke one more time,
I'm going out the door.

Visual vs. Verbal

Contrary to what many people believe, movies are not primarily dependent upon dialogue. More than once I have heard writers say, "I'm great at dialogue, so I should be a terrific filmwriter." It is true that dialogue constitutes about 40 percent of a script. However, almost everyone who teaches, writes, or makes movies stresses the paramount importance (no pun intended) of the visual element in film.

What we recall most clearly from films are visual images. As for film dialogue, we tend to remember the short, provocative statements, not the longer speeches that some aspiring writers believe constitutes cinematic conversation. What film dialogue do you recall? From *Casablanca, Gone with the Wind,* or some other special favorite, you may be able to quote numerous speeches. But from most films, you either cannot repeat any dialogue, or you remember only one or two particularly pithy, witty, or otherwise memorable lines.

Paddy Chayefsky, for instance, wrote wonderful dialogue. His scripts include *Marty, The Hospital, The Americanization of Emily,* and *Altered States.* Yet, even with all the tongue-in-cheek prowar speeches in *The Americanization of Emily* and the brilliantly captured repetitive statements of ennui in *Marty,* the only line that most of us are likely to remember from Chayefsky is Howard Beale's outburst in *Network* (all together now): "I'm mad as hell, and I'm not going to take it any more."

Let's consider a few more examples. From all the many Tarzan movies, what line(s) do you remember? What about the James Bond series? Clint Eastwood is a genius at creating memorable dialogue—go ahead, quote me some Eastwood—but from his films, do you remember the dialogue or the visuals? Would you even remember those few terrific lines if it weren't for the strong images that accompanied them?

Cut the film dialogue, and the images still play fresh and clear in your mind. The power and lasting impact of visuals is what makes film so extraordinary.

So we should ignore dialogue? No way. Dialogue adds a compelling element to film. Speech is available to the screenwriter, and at times speech can give information that cannot be shown, or it can help advance the plot.

Unfortunately, sometimes writers abuse dialogue to the extreme by making it the main mechanism that carries the story. The result is a script that may be as much as 70 to 80 percent discussion. That much dialogue leaves little room for you to write the directions that create the visuals that you must have on film.

Writing dialogue that is strong, succinct, and correctly formatted must be your goal. It is a vital element in the success of your screenplay.

A REVIEW OF THE RULES FOR DIALOGUE

1. Margins for dialogue are:
   A. Character cue—first letter at middle of page, horizontal space 41.
   B. Character speech—begin at horizontal space 28 and end at horizontal space 56 to 58.
   C. Parenthetical—first parenthesis at horizontal space 35.
2. Always single-space from the character cue to the character speech and single-space within the speech.
3. Single-space from the character cue to the rare parenthetical and then single-space to the character speech.
4. No matter what precedes it, always double-space to the character cue.
5. Never orphan a character cue. Always place the character cue on the same page as the speech.
6. Always cap but *do not underline* the character cue.

In part one of the following exercise, taken from Frank McEvoy's "The Shroud Trinity," I have inserted several errors in dialogue as well as errors in spacing. Go through these pages and edit them using the guidelines you have just learned. Then in part two compare your corrections with the same scene presented correctly as the author wrote it. An asterisk indicates where corrections have been made.

Your corrections may not agree with Frank's in all respects. But the important questions to consider are did you use correct spacing and did you, with a minimum of words, preserve the essence of what was said.

Redwine creeps up to the convent window. He looks around the wall for some way to creep up to the second floor.

CONVENT WALL

There is an ornate rain downspout coming down the wall.

REDWINE

Mike examines the downspout before hoisting himself up on the pipe, a pipe which makes many ominous noises in protest. Slowly, he makes his way up the pipe to the window.

He fumbles with the exterior window handle. The window pops open, almost making him fall. With a flawed gymnast's skill, he manages to pull himself into the room.

INT. SISTER'S REC ROOM

Redwine lands headfirst on the oriental carpeting right inside the window. He lands hard. He gingerly stands up, brushes himself off, then turns and closes the window.

As he latches the window, a figure comes up behind him, puts a hand over Redwine's mouth.

                        REDWINE
                       (Angrily)
              "What's going on?"

                  MARY MARGARET

          Quiet, Mike! If anyone finds us

          here, I get thrown out of the

          order.

                                        (CONTINUED)

                         MIKE
               (Annoyed but not exasperated)
          I still have no idea what you're up
          to. This isn't a detective show on
          TV, you realize. Why did you get
          me to come here at this
          Godforsaken hour? What time is it
          anyway?

                    MARY MARGARET
                       (bored)
          It's ten after midnight.

                       REDWINE
          Twelve-ten and we're out mucking
          around like Magnum P.I. or
          something. I'm a member of the
          police force, in case you hadn't
          noticed. That's long hours at work,
          where I need some sleep. Maybe
          they don't do that on TV, but in
          real life...

                    MARY MARGARET
          I got you here because of Sister
          Eleanor.

                       REDWINE
          She's dead and gone, if you hadn't
          noticed.

                    MARY MARGARET
          Just before she died, SisterEleanor
          told me something.

                                        (CONTINUED)

                         REDWINE
                        (smirking)
                    And just what was that
                    "something?"

                         MARY MARGARET
                    That she always spoke words
                    plain, honest, and true.

MARY MARGARET

Looks out the window. She frowns.

                         REDWINE
                        (concerned)
                    What's wrong.

                         MARY MARGARET
                    I don't know.

                         REDWINE
                    You look as though something's
                    wrong...

                         MARY MARGARET
                        (whispering)
                    Do you know if you were followed?

                         REDWINE
                    Followed? That's a dumb idea.

                         MARY MARGARET

                    Well, uh, if you haven't the least

                    clue if you've been followed, it

                    seems to me that the possibility

                    exists.

                         REDWINE
                        bored
                    What else is the matter?

                         MARY MARGARET
                    It's just that this whole thing
                    seems to be a simple, chaotic,
                    stinking mess.

                                        (CONTINUED)

                              REDWINE
                    I have a small, insignificant, minor

                    question.

                          MARY MARGARET
                    What's that?

                              REDWINE

                    Where's Shea in all this? He's part

                    of this group.

                          MARY MARGARET
                    Oh, I forgot..........

REC ROOM

Mary Margaret pulls a small flashlight out of her pocket. Motioning to
Redwine to follow her, she crosses the large room to the wet bar.

She reaches for a large plastic tumbler with "Washington Redskins"
printed on it. She fills the tumbler with water from the sink. She
hands the tumbler to Redwine.

                              REDWINE
                    What's this for?

                          MARY MARGARET
                    You'll see.

BEHIND THE BAR

Mary Margaret stoops into the shadows. There is a shuffling, then she
manages to get Bartholomew up on the bar. Redwine is shocked for a
second, then throws the water in Bart's face.

Bart coughs and chokes himself awake. He glances between Redwine
and Mary Margaret.

                            BARTHOLOMEW
                    What are you two doing here?

                              REDWINE
                    What about you?

                                                    (CONTINUED)

60

MARY MARGARET
The monitors at the front door are notoriously lax at this house. It has a campus-wide reputation for having the best bar in town.

(CONTINUED)

EXT. CONVENT - MIDNIGHT

Redwine creeps up to the convent window. He looks around the wall for some way to creep up to the second floor.

CONVENT WALL

There is an ornate rain downspout coming down the wall.

REDWINE

Mike examines the downspout before hoisting himself up on the pipe, a pipe which makes many ominous noises in protest. Slowly, he makes his way up the pipe to the window.

He fumbles with the exterior window handle. The window pops open, almost making him fall. With a flawed gymnast's skill, he manages to pull himself into the room.

INT. SISTER'S REC ROOM

Redwine lands headfirst on the oriental carpeting right inside the window. He lands hard. He gingerly stands up, brushes himself off, then turns and closes the window.

As he latches the window, a figure comes up behind him, puts a hand over Redwine's mouth.

> MARY MARGARET
> *Quiet! If anyone finds us here, I
> get thrown out of the order.

> *REDWINE
> *What do you think you're doing?
> This isn't a detective show.

> MARY MARGARET
> Just before she died, Sister
> Eleanor told me to have us look in
> her drawer.

> REDWINE
> *What else did she say?

> *MARY MARGARET
> That she always spoke words
> plain, honest, and true.

MARY MARGARET

Looks out the window. She frowns.

(CONTINUED)

>   MARY MARGARET
>   *Do you know if you were
>   followed?

>   REDWINE
>   Followed? That's a dumb idea.

>   MARY MARGARET
>   *That's a no. It's just that I think
>   this whole thing's a mess.

>   REDWINE
>   *One small question. Where's Shea
>   in all this? He's part of this
>   group.

>   MARY MARGARET
>   * Oh, I forgot.

REC ROOM

Mary Margaret pulls a small flashlight out of her pocket. Motioning to Redwine to follow her, she crosses the large room to the wet bar.

She reaches for a large plastic tumbler with "Washington Redskins" printed on it. She fills the tumbler with water from the sink. She hands the tumbler to Redwine.

>   REDWINE
>   What's this for?

>   MARY MARGARET
>   You'll see.

BEHIND THE BAR

Mary Margaret stoops into the shadows. There is a shuffling, then she manages to get Bartholomew up on the bar. Redwine is shocked for a second, then throws the water in Bart's face.

Bart coughs and chokes himself awake. He glances between Redwine and Mary Margaret.

>   BARTHOLOMEW
>   What are you two doing here?

>   REDWINE
>   *What about you?

>   MARY MARGARET
>   *The monitors at the front door
>   are notoriously lax at this house.
>   It has a campus-wide reputation
>   for having the best bar in town.

                                                            (CONTINUED)

                         BART
              Why die to go to heaven when all
              you have to do is walk across
              campus and climb a drain?

                    MARY MARGARET
              Cut the crap, Bart. We have to
              check out Sister Eleanor's office.

INT. SISTER ELEANOR'S OFFICE

The three quietly enter the office. Bart goes to the bookcase near the
window to try to open the hidden door.

                         BART
              She was right, you know.

He springs the catch, and the bookcase swings open.

                    MARY MARGARET
              Right about what?

                         BART
              That picture of the cardinal is a
              homey touch.

INT. THE SHROUD WORKSHOP

The three enter and move to the desk. Mary Margaret opens the
center drawer; the stationery and supplies are all neatly organized.
The three spend some time searching all the drawers and looking
through papers.

                       REDWINE
              We're not thinking right. She said
              to look through her drawer, right?

                    MARY MARGARET
              And that she always said things
              plain, honest, and true.

                       REDWINE
              So we look.

BART

Plunks himself in Sister Eleanor's desk chair. He scratches his head,
then rubs his eyes.

                    MARY MARGARET
              Serves you right if you get a
              hangover. Look through the
              drawer.
                                              (CONTINUED)

                         BART
          I am. I see the drawer handle, and
          the letters inside, and her grade
          book with no A for me in it, and
          then more junk, and the back of
          the drawer.

REDWINE

Looks up from the searching he's doing.

                       REDWINE
          Then the inside desk wood, then
          the outside again.

BART

Leans forward, then pulls the desk drawer out and places it on the
floor. He puts his arm through the desk opening, searches a bit, then
pulls out a large manila envelope.

                         BART
          Well, she spoke plain, honest, and
          true. All we had to be be was
          Superman to see through the
          wood.

SHROUD WORK TABLE

The three have the envelope open on the desk. It contains a variety of
photos and a packet of handwritten material. Bart picks up one of the
written pieces and reads it.

                         BART
          Well, Sister sure wrote like a nun.
          I can read every word.

MARY MARGARET

Picks up another document and reads it.

                     MARY MARGARET
          "To the Shroud Trinity -- for that
          is who is reading this now. I am
          dead, but the Shroud lives on, as
          you three will see. If you are
          reading this, then you and the
          Shroud are all in mortal danger.
          Be watchful."

Bart and Mary Margaret look at Redwine.

                                              (CONTINUED)

                    REDWINE
            I'm on your side, remember?

                    MARY MARGARET
            Take a look at the first photo.

BART

Starts fishing through the photos on the table.

                    MARY MARGARET
            Marked number one, stupid. Well, I
            guess that means this document is
            original.

PHOTO NO. 1.

is of a slight, mustachioed man standing behind an old boxed camera.

                    MARY MARGARET
            This is Secundo Pia, the
            photographer of the Shroud.

PHOTO SPFX

Comes to life in sepia as Mary Margaret's voice fades into Sister
Eleanor's. Secundo Pia stands photographing a crowd of Turin
residents.

                    SISTER ELEANOR (V.O.)
            Uncle Secundo was a genius in his
            own right. He developed a large
            number of photographic processes
            that revolutionized photography in
            Italy.

SECUNDO WITH THE CARDINAL

The two are meeting in the cardinal's baroque palace. Secundo nods.

                    SISTER ELEANOR (V.O.)
            So it was logical that the cardinal
            would ask that the Shroud be
            photographed during the 1903
            exposition.

SECUNDO IN THE TURIN CATHEDRAL

Secudo examines the exposed Shroud, measuring it, experimenting with lighting techniques.

SECUNDO PHOTOGRAPHING THE SHROUD

The photographer, in shirtsleeves and looking stressed, takes picture after picture of the Shroud.

> SISTER ELEANOR (V.O.)
> And it was he who first looked
> upon the face of the Lord, seen
> again after two thousand years.

SECUNDO IN DARKROOM

Pia takes a wet glass plate out of the developing bath, shakes it off, then holds it up to the light. His mouth drops open, and he drops the plate, smashing it to pieces.

CARDINAL'S PALACE

The cardinal and other clerics are arguing hotly. There is high emotion on every side.

CHAPTER
6

Dialogue, the Sequel

Movie talk is not cheap. So for a writer, overdependence on and overwriting of dialogue carries a price, usually the rejection of his or her screenplay.

When to Use Dialogue in Your Script

To assess when and how much dialogue is needed, it is essential to keep in mind what film dialogue accomplishes. Dialogue gives the reader information or characterization that *cannot be displayed visually,* or it shows conflict, thereby advancing the plot. Any other use of dialogue is superfluous.

Many writers use dialogue when a picture is or could be worth a great many words. For instance, suppose a scene opens in a blizzard. Would the stronger opening be:

INT. HOUSE - DAY

George enters. He shakes snow from his hat and fake-fur parka, then rubs his hands together.

```
                    GEORGE
        What a blizzard out there! Trees
        are all iced over, wires are down
        everywhere, nothing's moving on
        the street.
```

or

EXT. STREET - DAY

Mountainous snowdrifts cover the landscape. Broken off, ice-laden tree limbs lie scattered about. Downed power lines CRACKLE on the white, empty streets.

INT. HOUSE

George enters. He shakes snow from his hat and fake-fur parka, then rubs his hands together.

Obviously, the latter opening is stronger. It gives the information visually, rendering George's speech unnecessary.

Talking Heads

If you have read books on scriptwriting, you have run across the term "talking heads." The term does not refer to a rock group but to scenes in a filmscript where two or more characters talk endlessly. No matter how witty the banter, characters chatting incessantly—which may play well in live theater or even on television—generally kills a film.

One of my students, who initially wrote page after page of talking heads, led me to develop a rule of thumb to help solve this problem. You should write no more than one page of unbroken dialogue per scene. (And I don't mean that you can merely stick one or two lines of direction between two paragraphs of dialogue and then continue the dialogue for another page.) This suggestion helped my student purge unnecessary dialogue and include only vital speech.

Many beginning writers tend to make individual character speeches too long. To help minimize this problem, keep most speeches to no more than four lines. Admittedly, limits of four lines per speech and of one page of continuous dialogue per scene are arbitrary ones. But in the process of imposing those limits, my students are forced to recognize and to cut excess verbiage. After making these cuts, a student frequently realizes that his or her characters' speeches are stronger.

Creating Good Film Dialogue

Movie talk differs from that of real life and from that of television and plays in one huge aspect. Film dialogue is not naturalistic. Obviously, film dialogue will not be entirely natural because it is used only to show conflict or to give the reader information and characterization that cannot be displayed visually. Beyond that, film dialogue is not naturalistic in that it is free of little speech fillers, is devoid of small talk, and is mostly short and pithy. Creating good "film speak" usually requires dialogue surgery.

How do you perform this surgery? Fillers such as "well," "sure," "uh," "yeah," "gee," "of course," "like," "hey," "yo," "you know," "oh," and similar phrases add nothing to speech but excess words. They should be eliminated. If *one* of your characters distinguishes him or herself by the use of such phrases, this rule does not apply to that character.

Use of what I call redundant prepositions does nothing for your script but lengthen the dialogue. Again, unless the use of redundant prepositions is a trait of a particular character, you should avoid them.

> PROFESSOR GEORGE
> I discovered early on in this
> course that she had talent.

> DEPARTMENT HEAD CARL
> Later on, we went to her place.

> PRINCIPAL SAL
> Before I could do a thing, he
> started up the car.

I could continue on—I mean, continue—but I believe you get the point. How does "early on" or "later on" differ from "early" or "later"? Doesn't "started up" mean the same as "started"?

"But," I hear you think, "that's the way people talk." True, that is the way people talk. But what, pray tell, does *naturalism* have to do with movies? The answer is almost nothing.

Always cut the "hello" and "good-bye" in telephone conversations or chance meetings. What do such naturalisms add to information or plot? That's right, nothing.

To eliminate unnecessary chatter in your script, remember that film characters do not involve themselves in small talk. If a scene includes a doorman of an apartment building, our character does not stop to chat about the weather, the events of the day, or the health and well-being of the doorman's three Rottweilers. In fact, the doorman will be addressed only to advance the plot:

> CHARLOTTE
> Please give this package to Turner
> when he comes by.

or give information:

> CHARLOTTE
> I'll be gone several days so my
> usual house-sitter will be here.

You should not use someone's name in dialogue over and over and over and over and over and... you get the idea:

> GEORGE
> Did you take the letter to the post
> office, Tom?

> FRANCIS
> Yeah, Tom, I thought you were
> going to the post office for us.

> SAM
> You said you were going, Tom. I
> can't believe you forgot.

> LIBBY
> Gee, Tom, it wasn't like the post
> office was out of your way.

It might, at first thought, seem more dramatic to use a person's name. But when such sentences are spoken, the constant use of another person's name sounds awkward, strained, and artificial. Certainly you can use a character's name to establish who he or she is. You might also use a character's name when the character being addressed is part of a group. But in most instances the use of someone's name adds nothing to your scene but excess words.

You may be thinking, "Characters on TV, in superb shows such as 'Murphy Brown,' use fillers and names constantly." That's true. But TV is smaller, more intimate. Story and dialogue are usually closer to theater than to film. A movie has two hours or less to tell its story, rather than several weeks or even years. Using fillers and names usurps vital time.

Another problem that plagues writers is the tendency to repeat information. The cure is simple. Once you have said:

> DETECTIVE GEORGE
> Before we go after a suspect, we'll
> have to wait for the lab tests.

you do not later need:

                    DETECTIVE GEORGE
        We'll have a better idea about who
        the murderer is when the lab
        results come back.

or further:

                    DETECTIVE GEORGE
        The lab test could answer a lot of
        questions about who did this.

and just to make sure the audience did not miss it:

                    DETECTIVE GEORGE
        The lab tests could really pinpoint
        the murderer.

You laugh. But I do it, you do it, my guess is the best in Hollywood do it. The difference is that the best remove such foolishness long before the script is submitted.

In dialogue less is definitely more. Always ask yourself, "Is this speech absolutely necessary?" The great majority of the time it is not. It is amazing how much information can be conveyed in just a few short, but well-crafted sentences.

In part one of the following exercise, taken from Betty Blackburn's "As the Wind Is," I have inserted several errors in the use of dialogue. Go through these pages and edit them using the guidelines you have just learned. Then in part two compare your corrections with the same scene presented correctly as the author wrote it. An asterisk indicates where corrections have been made.

Your corrected version may not agree with Betty's version in all respects. But the important question to consider is, "Did you edit the fillers, small talk, and other useless verbiage from the dialogue?"

EXT. LONGBOAT/SEA - DAY

Richard, Adam, and Giaia are in a longboat loaded with kegs. Adam and Giaia row toward a large ship.

> RICHARD
> Could she have taken us, Adam?

> ADAM
> Well, yeah, It's Blackbeard's ship.

RICHARD

Richard narrows his eyes.

> RICHARD
> Blackbeard. Feared more by
> sailors than Neptune himself. A
> man who fears no one or no thing.

BACK TO SCENE

The longboat pulls alongside a rope ladder which hangs from the ship's side. Richard, first to stand, takes hold of the rope and looks up.

RICHARD'S POV

Above, a massive head, with matted hair and plaited beard tied in tails with little ribbons, hangs over the rail. Two deep-set eyes peer out of the tangled mass and look down at Richard.

From deep inside this mass comes a rumble, then a roar of guttural laughter. Below the head on the ship's side the name, *The Adventure*.

The head disappears.

EXT. DECK OF THE ADVENTURE - DAY

The main deck of *The Adventure* is similar to but larger than the *Revenge's* deck. There is a larger cabin area with quarter-deck above. There is a brazier with a smoldering fire on the main deck near where BLACKBEARD sits on the capstan surrounded by his beardless crew.

(CONTINUED)

Among his crew there is CUTTER, who has a wooden leg, HANDS, who has one hand. There is a small, wiry man CHIPS, with a weathered face who grins, and FLING, a tall gaunt man who stares with crazed eyes.

Blackbeard's LIEUTENANT, a swarthy, silent man, stands beside him.

Blackbeard is a giant of a man, strong, fierce, satanic. He wears a bandolier with two pistols, a powder horn, assorted daggers and a cutlass in a wide belt. He wears a hat and kerchief. He looks at Richard, amused.

Adam and Giaia step forward to stand on each side of Richard.

                    RICHARD
          So you're the famous and
          notorious pirate Blackbeard that
          I've heard so much about.

                    BLACKBEARD
          I am that. And it's good that ye
          know of me.

                    RICHARD
          Everyone who has ventured to sea
          knows of you. They speak your
          name with...

                    BLACKBEARD
          ... with terror, Captain.

                    RICHARD
          Yes, with terror and a hope that
          you will not live very long. But a
          fear that you probably will.

                    BLACKBEARD
          Ye bring comfortable news,
          Captain. Rum all out. Our company
          somewhat sober.

                    RICHARD
          We share our booty, when asked.
          Since you asked us, we have kegs
          of rum that we brought with us.

Blackbeard's crewmen haul kegs over the side. Blackbeard notices Giaia.

                    BLACKBEARD
          Hey, yo, your cannibal there, does
          he have a Christian name?

                                        (CONTINUED)

74

>   RICHARD
>   Uh, he's neither cannibal nor
>   Christian. His name is Giaia.

Blackbeard's crew slashes at the kegs with cutlasses and knocks the
tops in and dips hands in, slosh and spill.

>   BLACKBEARD
>   Save a keg or two to swab the
>   deck. T'will do till we get
>   medicines.

Blackbeard looks at Richard's uniform.

>   BLACKBEARD
>   So, Captain of the ship *Revenge*,
>   whence came you to pirating?

>   RICHARD
>   Major Farrar of His Majesty's
>   Colonial Forces.

>   BLACKBEARD
>   I see. So when young you had the
>   wherewithal to buy a commission.
>   Your humour of going a-pirating, a
>   disorder of the mind... A nagging
>   wife?

(CONTINUED)

EXT. LONGBOAT/SEA - DAY

Richard, Adam, and Giaia are in a longboat loaded with kegs. Adam and Giaia row toward a large ship.

                    RICHARD
        Could she have taken us, Adam?

                    ADAM
        *It's Blackbeard's ship.

RICHARD

Richard narrows his eyes.

                    RICHARD
        *Blackbeard.

BACK TO SCENE

The longboat pulls alongside a rope ladder which hangs from the ship's side. Richard, first to stand, takes hold of the rope and looks up.

RICHARD'S POV

Above, a massive head, with matted hair and plaited beard tied in tails with little ribbons, hangs over the rail. Two deep-set eyes peer out of the tangled mass and look down at Richard.

From deep inside this mass comes a rumble, then a roar of guttural laughter. Below the head on the ship's side the name, *The Adventure.*

The head disappears.

EXT. DECK OF THE ADVENTURE - DAY

The main deck of *The Adventure* is similar to but larger than the *Revenge's* deck. There is a larger cabin area with quarter-deck above. There is a brazier with a smoldering fire on the main deck near where BLACKBEARD sits on the capstan surrounded by his beardless crew.

                                        (CONTINUED)

Among his crew there is CUTTER, who has a wooden leg, HANDS, who has one hand. There is a small wiry man CHIPS, with a weathered face who grins, and FLING, a tall gaunt man who stares with crazed eyes.

Blackbeard's LIEUTENANT, a swarthy, silent man, stands beside him.

Blackbeard is a giant of a man, strong, fierce, satanic. He wears a bandolier with two pistols, a powder horn, assorted daggers and a cutlass in a wide belt. He wears a hat and kerchief. He looks at Richard, amused.

Adam and Giaia step forward to stand on each side of Richard.

                    BLACKBEARD
          * Ye bring comfortable news,
          Captain. Rum all out. Our company
          somewhat sober.

                    RICHARD
          * We share our booty, when asked.

Blackbeard's crewmen haul kegs over the side. Blackbeard notices Giaia.

                    BLACKBEARD
          * Your cannibal there, does he
          have a Christian name?

                    RICHARD
          * He's neither cannibal nor
          Christian. His name is Giaia.

Blackbeard's crew slashes at the kegs with cutlasses and knocks the tops in and dips hands in, slosh and spill.

                    BLACKBEARD
          Save a keg or two to swab the
          deck. T'will do till we get
          medicines.

Blackbeard looks at Richard's uniform.

                    BLACKBEARD
          So, Captain of the ship *Revenge*,
          whence came you to pirating?

                    RICHARD
          Major Farrar of His Majesty's
          Colonial Forces.

                                        (CONTINUED)

                    BLACKBEARD
          When young you had the wherewithal
          to buy a commission. Your humour of
          going a pirating, a disorder of the
          mind... A nagging wife?

Richard turns away.

                    BLACKBEARD
          Life on the sea is hell.

                    RICHARD
          And on land worse.

                    BLACKBEARD
          Aye, ye can be hanged for stealing
          a shilling. Why not try for a
          fortune, eh?

He pauses.

                    BLACKBEARD
                  (continuing)
          As to wives, I've had thirteen...
          passed them on to the crew.

Blackbeard snaps his finger at Hands, who goes to the brazier and
picks out a stick burning at one end, takes it and holds it, standing by
Blackbeard.

Blackbeard opens his powder horn and sprinkles a little gunpowder
into his cup. He raises the cup.

                    BLACKBEARD
          To vengeance and a short life of
          ease.

Blackbeard holds the cup under the burning stick Hands holds. The cup
fizzes and smokes. He drinks it down with a quick gulp.

                    BLACKBEARD
          We'll keep the company hot, damn
          hot, and all will go well... Major,
          shall we get to know each other?

Blackbeard gestures to the crew.

                    BLACKBEARD
                  (continuing)
          Get us three pots of brimstone to
          the hold and light the brimstone.

                                              (CONTINUED)

The crew watches Blackbeard as two of them comply slowly.

Blackbeard takes long wicks from his pocket, lights them from Hands's burning stick, and pokes them under his hat.

> BLACKBEARD
> I propose that we make a hell of
> our own and try how long we can
> bear it.

Blackbeard stands. He is a head taller than anyone. He turns to Richard with a swagger. Tendrils of smoke from the wicks curl around his eyes and matted hair.

Two crewmen open the hatch to the hold. Black and yellow smoke billows out. Blackbeard peers in and looks to Richard.

Richard stands immobile then suddenly, galvanized, he moved toward the hold.

Blackbeard walks to meet him and takes his arm. He escorts Richard toward the hatch with mock graciousness.

> BLACKBEARD
> Not a hail of flying splinters,
> not flailing cutlasses nor the...
> dead reckoning of gangrene...
> but a hell of our own making...
> but a hell of our own making...

Blackbeard roars with laughter. Blackbeard stops at the hatch and with a low bow

> BLACKBEARD
> (continuing)
> After you, Captain.

They disappear below in swirls of smoke.

Adam and Giaia's eyes meet across the hatch. Blackbeard's crew crowds in a circle around the hatch, partially obscured by spiraling smoke.

INT. HOLD OF THE ADVENTURE - DAY

Swirling smoke reveals Blackbeard's impassive face with closed eyes, spread nostrils breathing shallowly.

Richard's face is revealed near Blackbeard's. He squints through the smoke. Blackbeard's eyes open and stare at Richard, who stares back.

                                                        (CONTINUED)

Blackbeard takes his kerchief off and holds it up for Richard to see as he fills the kerchief with powder from the powder horn. He takes a lighted wick from under his hat and sticks it in the kerchief and ties the kerchief ends.

> BLACKBEARD
> We'll up the ante.

Richard stares at the sparking wick in Blackbeard's hand.

Smoke drifts across their faces. They cough and breathe in spasms.

Blackbeard's cough turns to a roar, then gasping laughter. The burning wick sputters and sparks as smoke obscures their faces.

EXT. DECK OF THE ADVENTURE

Adam, Giaia, and Blackbeard's crew circle the hatch and listen to the o.s. COUGHS and SPASMS. The COUGHS and SPASMS cease.

Giaia steps forward. Adam restrains him. They wait.

The hatch opens from below. Smoke billows forth, scatters, and reveals first Blackbeard, then Richard.

Blackbeard chokes and wheezes. He roars with laughter. He staggers to the rail and throws the smoking kerchief overboard.

There is muffled o.s. BOOM. Spray hits the ship's deck.

Richard hangs over another section of the rail beside Adam and Giaia.

> BLACKBEARD
> Next time we shall see who can
> swing the longest on the string
> without being throttled.

Blackbeard stares at his crew. Crewmen cringe under his stare. Blackbeard roars.

> BLACKBEARD
> Don't forget who I am!

Blackbeard gulps air, turns to Richard, speaks softly.

> BLACKBEARD
> Don't forget who I am.

(CONTINUED)

CHAPTER
7

Capitalization, Abbreviation, Dashes,
and Ellipses

Capitalization, abbreviations, dashes, and ellipses are little things that mean a lot. When properly used in a script, these small details set apart the good from the bad and the ugly.

Capitalization

In scripts, words written in all caps highlight important information. Slugs and character cues—discussed in chapters 2, 3, and 4—are good examples. There are also certain words in directions that should appear in all caps.

AD LIB, which is general, extemporaneous chatter among a group of people, should always be written in all caps.

As he wanders from room to room, he hears AD LIB conversation from the various partygoers.

MOS is a German term meaning "without sound." It can appear in slugs or directions. It is always in all caps:

The two men talk MOS.

Book and song titles should be all capped:

He buys a copy of the FILMWRITER'S FORMAT BOOK to learn Hollywood
script format.

It is best *not* to specify a particular song unless it is in public domain—an artistic work which was never copyrighted or for which the copyright has expired—or musical artist in your screenplay. The cost of royalties for music and payment to artists can be prohibitive and can kill a producer's interest in your work. Moreover, while you want music by Red, Hot, and Slime, the producer prefers Mutant Madness and perhaps downgrades your screenplay because of your obviously inferior musical tastes.

Sounds are capped if they are not a result of the actions of a person or event on screen. Cap the actual word that represents the noise:

He hears the BUZZ of the alarm clock.

The shrill CHIRP of the giant crickets SHATTERED the window.

If the noise results from action on screen, however, it does not need to be highlighted:

He shatters the bottle against the railing.

In general, it is not necessary to cap visual props. Visual props such as signs and billboards or props such as a candle that will not blow out, however, might be capped to alert the crew that these special props will be needed:

The door sign read GARY GUNN, DETECTIVE.

While character cues are written all in caps, in directions, characters' names appear in upper- and lower-case type *except* when a character is introduced. At his or her first appearance, the character's full name should appear in all caps:

CLIME DONNER, about six feet, mid-fifties, muscular and fit, enters the bar
flashing the grin the devil surely wore when he first discovered mankind.

Clime surveys the room, then ambles to a corner table.

Abbreviations

In scripts, certain terms are always abbreviated. Some, including POV, INT., EXT., SPFX, we looked at in chapter 4. However, there are a few more we need to note.

Background is always abbreviated b.g.:

```
He saw something move in the b.g.
```

If b.g. begins a sentence, it is written B.g.

Foreground is always shortened to f.g.:

```
The dog barks in the f.g. as Shirley goes back to investigate the strange
noises coming from inside the house.
```

If f.g. begins a sentence, it is written F.g.

off screen (O.S.) and voice over (V.O.)

The term off screen is frequently used in scripts. Off screen, always abbreviated o.s. or O.S., signifies that the character speaking or the cause of a particular noise, though nearby, is not shown in the scene.

In using off screen in dialogue, the writer has placed the speaking character out of the shot, even though he or she is nearby. While the shot shows us another character, the character speaking might be across a table, in another room of the house, or outside while the listener is inside.

To use off screen in dialogue, write it in caps and enclose it in parentheses, one horizontal space over from the character cue:

```
                    TODD (O.S.)
            Come on, open the door.
```

An off screen speech is also indicated if your shot is from the speaker's POV:

```
SARA'S POV

Gump, the St. Bernard, bounds out to her. She pets and hugs him.

                    SARA (O.S.)
            Look at how large you've gotten.
```

When off screen is used in direction, use lower-case type and drop the parentheses:

`Katz hears strange VOICES o.s.`

If off screen begins a sentence in direction, the *o* is capped and the *s* is lower-case:

`O.s. Slater hears the cycle ROAR away.`

The term voice over is often confused with off screen. Use voice over in the following cases:

1. When a character who cannot be in the shot speaks. (Have you ever noticed that every time in TV or film someone picks up a letter, it is always read in the voice of the person who wrote it?):

> LITTLE JOHNNY (V.O.)
> Dear Dad, Mommy offered me part
> of her stock portfolio and a couple
> of shopping centers to stay with
> her. But I'm sure I could be
> persuaded to come live with you
> instead. Perhaps we could discuss
> one of your estates and that NFL
> franchise.

2. When the character's voice is transmitted over an electronic medium, such as a telephone or television:

> NEWS ANCHOR (V.O.)
> The vice president said again that
> it was his golf score and not his IQ
> that somehow got printed on those
> college records.

3. For narration, whether the character speaking is on screen or not.

> CHARACTER (V.O.)
> He had all the subtlety of Mr. T
> and the looks of Karl Malden's
> hat.

Also notice that when voice over is used with the character cue, it is written in all caps and enclosed by parenthesis:

In direction, if v.o. begins a sentence, they *v* is capped and the *o* is in lower-case type. If v.o. falls within the sentence, both letters are lower-case.

84

Though Larry was gone, she continued to hear his v.o. on the telephone.

```
                    LARRY (V.O.)
          No, no, no, no, no, well, okay!
```

Dashes and Ellipses

Many times in film, speeches are interrupted. These interruptions are indicated by an ellipsis (...) or by a dash (--). If the speaker is interrupted by another person, use a dash:

```
                    SALLY
          And I expect to find--

                    COLIN
          It ain't here, Sugar.
```

However, when a speaker pauses:

```
                    SALLY
          This isn't... I mean I didn't think
          you'd be here.
```

the pause is signified by an ellipsis. The first dot is placed immediately after the final letter of the last word before the interruption. If the speech continues within the same dialogue, a space is left between the third dot and the letter that begins the continuing speech.

In scripts a dash is indicated by two hyphens. Unlike in standard prose, there is a space on either side of the dash:

```
Hank -- the man Dave swore he had seen near the cabin that night -- did not
seem to exist.
```

Missing one or two of these items will certainly not eliminate your screenplay from anyone's consideration. However, doing everything correctly will allow the reader to confirm that you are a professional. If you have the details correct, it is certainly reasonable to expect that the rest is also in marvelous shape.

A REVIEW OF THE RULES FOR CAPITALIZATION, ABBREVIATIONS, DASHES, AND ELLIPSES

Capitalization:

In direction, always cap:

1. AD LIB.
2. MOS (without sound).
3. Book and song titles.
4. Sounds that are not a result of the actions of a person or event on screen.
5. Special visual props.
6. A character's full name when first introduced. Subsequently, use upper- and lower-case type for the character's name.

Abbreviations:

1. Background as b.g.
2. Foreground as f.g.

If either b.g. or f.g. begins a sentence, cap the first letter.

3. Off Screen in direction as o.s.
4. Voice Over in direction as v.o.

If off screen or voice over begins a sentence in direction, write the first letter in caps.

If you use off screen or voice over with the character cue, cap the term and place it in parentheses one space over from the character cue.

Interruptions and pauses in dialogue:

1. When a speaker is interrupted by another person, use a dash. In direction and dialogue, always leave a space on either side of a dash.
2. When a speaker pauses, use ellipses. If the speech continues after the ellipses, a space is left between the third dot and the letter beginning the continued speech.

In part one of the following exercise, taken from Flo Cameron's "Dark Dreams," I have inserted several errors in the use of capitalization, abbreviation, dashes, and ellipses. Go through these pages and edit them using the guidelines you have learned. Then in part two compare your corrections with the same scene presented correctly as the author wrote it. An asterisk indicates where corrections have been made.

int. Dawson's office - 6:15 P.M.

at JFK High School. Tidy stacks of papers adorn the steel desk. School pennants decorate the drab, beige walls. The phone rings.

The clock on the wall

reads 6:15. The powerful, metronomelike ticking of the clock can be heard, Spfx, throughout the scene.

INT. high school hallway

outside the principal's office. The hallway is lined with a sea of student lockers.

LOCKERS

smeared with bloody handprints.

POOL OF BLOOD

on the floor. Lying in the pool of blood is a female body, face down, dead.

SIGN ON BULLETIN BOARD

near the end of the hallway, which reads: "prom committee meeting 3 p.m. sharp! ROOM 213."

INT. CLASSROOM 213

Allison is slumped over the desk.

A nail polish bottle on the desk has tipped over; red nail polish drips down the side of the desk. Falling into a pool of blood beneath Allison's chair.

                                                        CUT TO:

WATER

drips from a discolored pipe that runs from the floor up the wall and across the ceiling.

INT. BRIDGE CLUB - 7 P.M.

A large, drab room in which groups of four play bridge in air thick with cigar and cigarette haze. The pipe dripping water is visible in the corner.

The bridge players addlib bridge conversation, such as: "three no-trump"; "play a little club"; "ruff the heart"; and "who's dummy?" The players drink cocktails and argue bridge quietly at their tables.

A BEEPER wails. A hush falls over the room. The players stare at the man with the beeper.

DET. BILL MUNDES, a big man in his mid forties who barely fits into his archaic, checked sport jacket, puts down his highball, fumbles for his beeper, and turns it off. He speaks to his bridge partner, an elegant middle-aged woman.

                    DET. MUNDES
          Sorry, hon.

His partner flings down her cards.

                    BRIDGE PARTNER
          You're impossible! I'm getting a
          new partner--

INT. HALLWAY

outside the tournament room. Det. Mundes speaks on a pay telephone.

                    Det. Mundes
          Mother of God! I'll be right there...

                                        CUT TO:

EXT. LANDER'S HOUSE - NIGHT

Two uniformed police officers talk ms. to Sarah. The porch light illuminates the trio.

THE FLASHING LIGHT

on the police cruiser in front of the Lander's house disrupts the natural neighborhood calm.

                                        MATCH CUT:

A RIVER OF FLASHING LIGHTS

on the police cruisers in front of JFK High School broadcasts the presence of unfolding disaster and untold grief.

EXT. JFK HIGH SCHOOL - night

A scene of absolute chaos: ambulances, police cars, camera crews, flashing lights, and a curious crowd litter the front of the school. Floodlights cast an eerie, unnatural brightness against the dark night.

Police officers interview frightened students and parents. Police car RADIO noises and various crowd MUTTERINGS drown out individual conversations.

ON THE SCHOOL LAWN

a little girl and boy stand, engrossed in the carnival atmosphere. The girl holds the boy's hand as he licks a lollipop.

ANCHORWOMAN

using JFK High School as a backdrop.

                    ANCHORWOMAN -- V.O.
                This is Jane Whitcomb, WGTV
                Channel 8, live at John F. Kennedy
                High School in McLean, where two
                high school students were fatally
                wounded tonight by an unknown
                assailant...

                                            MATCH CUT:

ANCHORWOMAN

on a television set which is tuned to WGTV.

                    ANCHORWOMAN (o.s.)
                The identities of the students are
                being withheld pending notification
                of the next of kin.

89

INT. DEN - NIGHT

Scottie watches the WGTV broadcast. Sarah, in the background, talks in hushed tones to Lena, the maid. Scottie, turns away from the T.V. and interrupts their conversation.

> SCOTTIE
> Mommy, is Tad okay?

David enters, carrying two coats. He approaches Lena.

> DAVID
> Thanks for staying with Scottie.

EXT. JFK HIGH SCHOOL - NIGHT

ANCHORWOMAN JANE WHITCOMB tries to interview Det. Mundes.

> ANCHORWOMAN
> Det. Mundes, can you tell us the
> identity of the slain students?

Det. Mundes slicks back a stray lock of hair.

> DET. MUNDES
> No, Jane, I can't. You'll have to
> excuse me, I'm very busy.

THE SCHOOL DOORS

open. A stretcher is carried out of the high school; the body is covered with a white sheet.

THE CROWD

gasps. Someone cries. The assorted camera crews swing around and focus their cameras on the stretcher as it's placed into an ambulance.

MARIEL KARALAK'S CAR

is parked close to the spot where it had been parked earlier. Dr. Dawson leans against Mariel's car, watching the commotion from a distance.

TAD'S PARKING SPACE

IS EMPTY.

* INT. DAWSON'S OFFICE - 6:15 P.M.

at JFK High School. Tidy stacks of papers adorn the steel desk. School pennants decorate the drab, beige walls. The phone RINGS.

* THE CLOCK ON THE WALL

reads 6:15. The powerful, metronomelike ticking of the clock can be heard, *SFX, throughout the scene.

* INT. HIGH SCHOOL HALLWAY

outside the principal's office. The hallway is lined with a sea of student lockers.

LOCKERS

smeared with bloody handprints.

POOL OF BLOOD

on the floor. Lying in the pool of blood is a female body, face down, dead.

SIGN ON BULLETIN BOARD

near the end of the hallway, which reads: *"PROM COMMITTEE MEETING 3 P.M. SHARP! ROOM 213."

INT. CLASSROOM 213

Allison is slumped over the desk.

A nail polish bottle on the desk has tipped over; red nail polish drips down the side of the desk, *falling into a pool of blood beneath Allison's chair.

CUT TO:

WATER

drips from a discolored pipe that runs from the floor up the wall and across the ceiling.

INT. BRIDGE CLUB - 7 P.M.

A large, drab room in which groups of four play bridge in air thick with cigar and cigarette haze. The pipe dripping water is visible in the corner.

The bridge players *AD LIB bridge conversation, such as: "three no-trump"; "play a little club"; "ruff the heart"; and "who's dummy?" The players drink cocktails and argue bridge quietly at their tables.

A BEEPER wails. A hush falls over the room. The players stare at the man with the beeper.

DET. BILL MUNDES, a big man in his mid forties who barely fits into his archaic, checked sport jacket, puts down his highball, fumbles for his beeper, and turns it off. He speaks to his BRIDGE PARTNER, an elegant middle-aged woman.

                    DET. MUNDES
          Sorry, hon.

His partner flings down her cards.

                    BRIDGE PARTNER
          You're impossible! I'm getting a
          new partner.*

INT. HALLWAY

outside the tournament room. Det. Mundes speaks on a pay telephone.

                    DET. MUNDES *
          Mother of God! I'll be right there.*

                                        CUT TO:

EXT. LANDERS' HOUSE - NIGHT

Two uniformed police officers talk * MOS to Sarah. The porch light illuminates the trio.

THE FLASHING LIGHT

on the police cruiser in front of the Landers' house disrupts the natural neighborhood calm.

                                        MATCH CUT:

A RIVER OF FLASHING LIGHTS

on the police cruisers in front of JFK High School broadcasts the presence of unfolding disaster and untold grief.

EXT. JFK HIGH SCHOOL - *NIGHT

A scene of absolute chaos: ambulances, police cars, camera crews, flashing lights, and a curious crowd litter the front of the school. Floodlights cast an eerie, unnatural brightness against the dark night.

Police officers interview frightened students and parents. Police car RADIO noises and various crowd MUTTERINGS drown out individual conversations.

ON THE SCHOOL LAWN

a little girl and boy stand, engrossed in the carnival atmosphere. The girl holds the boy's hand as he licks a lollipop.

ANCHORWOMAN

using JFK High School as a backdrop.

                    ANCHORWOMAN
          This is Jane Whitcomb, WGTV
          Channel 8, live at John F. Kennedy
          High School in McLean, where two
          high school students were fatally
          wounded tonight by an unknown
          assailant...

                                        MATCH CUT:

ANCHORWOMAN

on a television set which is tuned to WGTV.

                    ANCHORWOMAN *(V.O.)
          The identities of the students are
          being withheld pending notification
          of the next of kin.

INT. DEN - NIGHT

Scottie watches the WGTV broadcast. Sarah, in the b.g., talks in hushed tones to Lena, the maid. Scottie, turns away from the T.V. and interrupts their conversation.

                                        (CONTINUED)

CONTINUED:

                    SCOTTIE
          Mommy, is Tad okay?

David enters, carrying two coats. He approaches Lena.

                    DAVID
          Thanks for staying with Scottie.

                                        CUT TO:

EXT. JFK HIGH SCHOOL - NIGHT

ANCHORWOMAN JANE WHITCOMB tries to interview Det. Mundes.

                    ANCHORWOMAN
          Det. Mundes, can you tell us the
          identity of the slain students?

Det. Mundes slicks back a stray lock of hair.

                    DET. MUNDES
          No, Jane, I can't. You'll have to
          excuse me, I'm very busy.

THE SCHOOL DOORS

open. A stretcher is carried out of the high school; the body is covered
with a white sheet.

THE CROWD

gasps. Someone cries. The assorted camera crews swing around and
focus their cameras on the stretcher as it's placed into an ambulance.

MARIEL KARALAK'S CAR

is parked close to the spot where it had been parked earlier. Dr.
Dawson leans against Mariel's car, watching the commotion from a
distance.

TAD'S PARKING SPACE

* is empty.

Part Two

FINISHING
TOUCHES

CHAPTER
8

Fades and Cuts

Fades and cuts are those short, always-capped instructions that begin, advance, and end a full-length filmscript. Fades begin and end a script. Cuts perform two functions: They end one segment of your script—shot, scene, or sequence, and they signal a transition to the next. Since fades are simpler, we'll examine them first.

Fades

Fades consist of FADE IN: and FADE OUT. Period. Each is used only once in a filmscript. FADE IN: begins your screenplay. FADE OUT. ends your screenplay.

FADE IN:

You write FADE IN: in all caps, followed by a colon. Triple-space down from the title on page 1—not the title page—of your screenplay, and begin FADE IN: at 1.4 inches from the left edge of the paper, or space fourteen—the same margin as for slugs and directions. FADE IN: appears at *no* other place in a full-length filmscript:

So page 1 of the script might begin:

"THE OLD MAN AND THE BELTWAY"

FADE IN:

From FADE IN: you double-space to the opening slug. This is the only instance in a script in which you double-space to a slug line.

FADE OUT.

FADE OUT. marks the end of screenplay text. It is written in all caps and followed by a period. Double-spaced from your last direction or dialogue in the script, FADE OUT. begins at 6.1 inches from the left edge of the paper, or space sixty-one.

So the script might end:

Harry makes another mark on the dashboard. His twelfth day on the Capital Beltway. He looks down the highway and smiles for the first time since the eighth—or was it the ninth?—cargo spill closed the Beltway.

HARRY'S POV

The signpost ahead. His exit. But another sign informs:
RAMP CLOSED DUE TO CONSTRUCTION.

FADE OUT.

THE END

Cuts

Cuts are more complicated to use than fades. Cuts are the short, always-capped elements of the screenplay that tell a reader that a shot, scene, or sequence is finished and that a new shot, scene, or sequence is imminent.

If you have read scripts, you have seen several examples of cuts. These may have included JUMP CUT:, DISSOLVE TO:, FADE TO:, SLAM CUT:, etc. The differences among these terms are mostly in the writer's mind. Unless the writer is penning the screenplay for himself or herself to direct, the timing and type of cut will be determined by the film's director and/or editor.

A cut is a cut is a cut. In a screenplay, you need to use only two types of cuts. The first is CUT TO:; the second is MATCH CUT:.

Both cuts are capped and written as two words followed by a colon. Both cuts begin 6.1 inches, or sixty-one spaces, from the left edge of the page. Neither cut is underlined, and neither should *ever* be the first line on any page.

CUT TO:

Since CUT TO: is used more often than MATCH CUT:, let's focus on it first. CUT TO: tells the reader that one section is finished and a new one follows. Whether the scene ends with direction or dialogue, the writer double-spaces to the CUT TO:, then triple-spaces to the following slug.

An example of a scene ending with directions is:

This scene has just ended.

                                                            CUT TO:

SLUG

An example of a scene ending with dialogue is:

                          RICK
          We will end here so I have the last
          word.

                                                            CUT TO:

SLUG

The tradition has been to use CUT TO: after each scene, or even when there is a major change of time or place within a scene. However, there is reason to alter that custom. If you conclude each scene with a CUT TO:, you will have twenty to thirty of them in one screenplay. That means that you will have 100 to 150 lines in the script, nearly three full pages, of mostly empty space.

To avoid this problem, *employ cuts when there is a major change of place, time, and/or action.* Such changes usually do not take place within a scene, but they do happen at the end of some scenes and at the end of all sequences.

SEQUENCE

What is a sequence? Glad you asked. A sequence consists of consecutive scenes that center on a theme and/or action and, like a scene, contains a beginning, middle, and end.

In a Western, a gunfight between the hero and villain might be a scene or a sequence depending on the way it is written. Suppose you begin with the rogue calling out the hero. You continue with the hero's speech to his lady, the reaction of the townspeople to the impending duel, the verbal exchange between the hero and villain before the showdown, the showdown, and the immediate aftereffect.

You might write this segment as one scene. Or, if you chose to write it as a sequence, you would create several scenes for each change of action, i.e., the hero's speech to his lady; the reaction of the townspeople, etc.

Whichever way you decide to write it, suppose that after the gunfight you show a house hundreds of miles away where a small rancher defends his family and land against a wealthy, greedy neighbor. Use of a CUT TO: between the gunfight section and the rancher section would be appropriate. After all, you have changed location, time, theme, action, and characters. It is a major change and, therefore, would best be preceded by a CUT TO:.

MATCH CUT:

With a MATCH CUT, on the other hand, the writer uses a physical object to bridge shots, scenes, or sequences. Let's return to our Western. The rancher sends a telegram to the hero. (Obviously, our hero won the gunfight, or completing our hypothetical script would be more difficult.) Your script might read:

TELEGRAM

asking for our hero's help, is seen as the message is BEEPED over the wire.

MATCH CUT:

TELEGRAM

appears again.

EXT. RANCHER'S HOUSE - DAY

The hero, holding the telegram, knocks on the door of the rancher's house.

Through MATCH CUT:, we have in seconds shown a trip of hundreds of miles, the passing of several days, and the decision by the hero to help the underdog family. We have simply used the telegram as the object that bridged the gunfight scene(s) and the hero's arrival at the ranch.

In the example above, even though

EXT. RANCHER'S HOUSE - DAY

is the primary slug, the new scene begins with the slug:

TELEGRAM

This is the one exception to the rule that a primary slug always introduces a scene. If a new scene or sequence follows the rare MATCH CUT:, it will not begin with a primary slug.

You can also use MATCH CUT: within a scene. For instance, suppose you establish a scene that begins with a mother and her son at the zoo:

EXT. ZOO - MORNING

Mother and son watch seals swim underwater. Nearby, another small boy throws an object into the water.

WATER

The object causes ripples, obscuring the sight of seals gliding under the water.

If you want to show the day passing, you might then go to:

MATCH CUT:

WATER

Ripples spread over the surface.

ZOO - LATE AFTERNOON

The boy and his mother toss small chunks of bread to ducks that have gathered at the edge of the pond. The lowering sun casts the boy's and his mother's shadows across the water.

MATCH CUT: should not be overused, or its effectiveness will be lost. At most, use two or three per script.

A Review of the Rules for Fades and Cuts

FADE IN:

1) is used only to begin a full-length filmscript.
2) is written in all caps, followed by a colon (:).
3) is triple-spaced from the title on page one.
4) is begun at 1.4 inches from the left edge of the paper, or space fourteen.
5) is followed by double-spacing to the opening slug.

FADE OUT.

1) ends a screenplay.
2) is written in all caps and followed by a period.
3) is double-spaced from the last direction or dialogue in the screenplay.
4) is begun at 6.1 inches from the left edge of the paper, or space sixty-one.
5) is followed by THE END.

CUTS

1) The only cuts you need are CUT TO: and MATCH CUT:.
2) Use cuts to show a change of scene or sequence.
3) Start cuts at space sixty-one; write them in all caps, do not underline, and follow cuts with a colon.
4) Whether a cut is preceded by direction or dialogue, always double space to it and triple space to the following slug.
5) Never begin a page with a cut. You may, however, end a page with a cut.

Though fades and cuts do not have a major role in your screenplay, proper use of them helps make your pages look professional. Attention to details such as fades and cuts helps your screenplay stand out from all the others in that enormous pile of submitted scripts.

In part one of the following exercise, taken from Wanda Warner's "Bad Manners," I have inserted several errors in the use of fades and cuts. Go through these pages and edit them using the guidelines you have just learned. Then in part two compare your corrections with the same scene presented correctly as the author wrote it. An asterisk indicates where corrections have been made.

"BAD MANNERS"

fade in:

EXT. COURTHOUSE - WASHINGTON D.C. - AFTERNOON (PRESENT)

A stiff autumn breeze whips fallen leaves, sheets of newspapers, and other debris across the pavement.

People struggling with flyaway hair and skirts hurry down the sidewalk.

KEVIN BOOTH, a boyishly appealing divorce lawyer shy of thirty but of little else, sits on the dusty top step leading to the courthouse. He studies the activity on the sidewalk and street below.

MATCH CUT:

BELOW

A cab driver fumes as an elderly woman meticulously digs through her purse for the fare. A courier chains his bicycle to a parking meter.

Two middle-aged men with bulky briefcases argue so intensely that one fails to notice when litter blows against his trouser leg.

Two women with shapely legs rush by. Kevin focuses on the legs until they disappear behind a kid walking two mongrels.

CUT TO:

EXT. COURTHOUSE

Kevin squints into the sun. His button-down shirt and sports coat are slightly wrinkled; the tie's a poor choice.

MATT, Kevin's young legal assistant, runs out of the courthouse and hollers MOS to Kevin.

CUT TO:

(CONTINUED)

Kevin scoops up the bulky briefcase that had been lying out of view
behind him and rushes past Matt toward the courthouse door.

                                                          cut to:

MATT'S POV

Seat of Kevin's pants smudged from the step.

                                                          MATCH

BACK TO SCENE

Matt catches up to Kevin and whispers to him. Kevin stops, wipes off
his pants. Matt nods when most of the dirt disappears.

                                                          CUT TO

INT. COURTHOUSE

Kevin paces before a bespectacled black judge and a handful of
spectators.

                          KEVIN
               Your honor, Miss Tate...

Kevin motions to a stern-faced young lawyer, ELLEN TATE, who's
whispering to her client, a weary-eyed teenaged mother slumped in the
chair beside her.

                          KEVIN
                      (continuing)
               ... is correct that only three out of
               every ten patients at ARCAP beats
               his drug habit.

Kevin turns to his client, a well-groomed, fresh-faced young man in his
early twenties.

                          KEVIN
               My client is one of the successful
               three. All he wants with his son is
               one weekend a month.

The judge thumbs through the ARCAP report and unconsciously shakes
his head. Miss Tate smiles broadly. Kevin senses doom and quickly
improvises.

                                                    (CONTINUED)

> KEVIN
> If necessary, his parents will
> supervise the visits until the Court
> is fully convinced that he's ready
> for this.

The sudden suggestion stuns Kevin's young client. The judge leans back in his chair. There's a silence in the courtroom.

EXT. COURTHOUSE STEPS - DAY

Kevin, his client, and client's parents joyfully exit the courthouse. The client gratefully shakes Kevin's hand. Kevin, a pleased smile on his face, watches them get into a taxi.

                                                    FADE OUT TO:

"BAD MANNERS"

*FADE IN:

EXT. COURTHOUSE - WASHINGTON D.C. - AFTERNOON   (PRESENT)

A stiff autumn breeze whips fallen leaves, sheets of newspapers, and other debris across the pavement.

People struggling with flyaway hair and skirts hurry down the sidewalk and other debris across the pavement.

KEVIN BOOTH, a boyishly appealing divorce lawyer shy of thirty but of little else, sits on the dusty top step leading to the courthouse. He studies the activity on the sidewalk and street below.*

BELOW

A cab driver fumes as an elderly woman meticulously digs through her purse for the fare. A courier chains his bicycle to a parking meter.

Two middle-aged men with bulky briefcases argue so intensely that one fails to notice when litter blows against his trouser leg.

Two women with shapely legs rush by. Kevin focuses on the legs until they disappear behind a kid walking two mongrels.*

EXT. COURTHOUSE

Kevin squints into the sun. His button-down shirt and sports coat are slightly wrinkled; the tie's a poor choice.

MATT, Kevin's young legal assistant, runs out of the courthouse and hollers MOS to Kevin.

Kevin scoops up the bulky briefcase that had been lying out of view behind him and rushes past Matt toward the courthouse door.*

MATT'S POV

Seat of Kevin's pants smudged from the step.

BACK TO SCENE

Matt catches up to Kevin and whispers to him. Kevin stops, wipes off his pants. Matt nods when most of the dirt disappears.*

INT. COURTHOUSE

Kevin paces before a bespectacled black judge and a handful of spectators.

                    KEVIN
          Your honor, Miss Tate...

Kevin motions to a stern-faced young lawyer, ELLEN TATE, who's whispering to her client, a weary-eyed teenaged mother slumped in the chair beside her.

                    KEVIN
                 (continuing)
          ... is correct that only three out of
          every ten patients at ARCAP beats
          his drug habit.

Kevin turns to his client, a well-groomed, fresh-faced young man in his early twenties.

                    KEVIN
          My client is one of the successful
          three. All he wants with his son is
          one weekend a month.

The judge thumbs through the ARCAP report and unconsciously shakes his head. Miss Tate smiles broadly. Kevin senses doom and quickly improvises.

                    KEVIN
          If necessary, his parents will
          supervise the visits until the Court
          is fully convinced that he's ready
          for this.

The sudden suggestion stuns Kevin's young client. The judge leans back in his chair. There's a silence in the courtroom.

EXT. COURTHOUSE STEPS - DAY

Kevin, his client, and client's parents joyfully exit the courthouse. The client gratefully shakes Kevin's hand. Kevin, a pleased smile on his face, watches them get into a taxi.*

CHAPTER
9

Marginals

Fans of *Mad* magazine know marginals as the wickedly delightful cartoons found at the margins of the page. In scripts, however, marginals denote the small but significant items also found at the margins of the page. These items include *title, continueds, page numbers,* and **THE END**. Since the title and **THE END** are found only once each in the body of the screenplay, let's cover them first.

Writing the Title

On page 1 of the screenplay (this is not the title page, which we will cover in chapter 9), you write the title six lines—about one and one-eighth inches from the top edge of the paper. Center the title; write it in all caps; place quotation marks on either side. For example:

"FIVE AND DIME KIDS"

Using **THE END**

You write **THE END** on the last page of your screenplay. Place **THE END** six lines below FADE OUT. Center it; write it in all caps; underline it. You end your screenplay with:

FADE OUT.

THE END

Paginating the Screenplay

In a script, as in a standard prose work, a page number appears on every page but the first. Place the page number four to six lines from the top edge of the paper. Begin it 7.3 inches, or seventy-three spaces, from the left edge. It may be written in one of three ways. You may simply write the number:

23

You may follow the number by a period:

23.

You may precede and follow the number with hyphens:

-23-

If you choose the third method, place the first hyphen at space seventy-two.

The first and third methods are most often used for full-length filmscripts. Use of the number followed by a period is more common in sitcom scripts.

Placing the CONTINUED

The marginal most complicated to use is CONTINUED. You have probably noticed CONTINUED in screenplays you have read. Sometimes CONTINUED appears at the top of the page, written as:

CONTINUED:

Sometimes CONTINUED is at the bottom of the page, written as:

(CONTINUED)

Many times CONTINUED shows up at both the top and bottom of the page. At other times CONTINUED is not on the page at all. So how the &#%@ do you know when to use CONTINUED?

There is a guideline for the proper use of CONTINUED at the top of the page. That rule is: Except for page one, the top of each page in a screenplay begins with either a CONTINUED or a slug.

The slug shows that you have begun a new shot. The CONTINUED shows that the *shot* you are writing is ongoing. Say again! Okay.

In chapter 2, I described the difference between a shot and a scene. A shot is _____. Therefore, each slug indicates a new shot.

If you end a page, but the shot that you are writing has not ended, then the next page is a continuation of the same shot. To show the reader that the shot is continuing, you write CONTINUED on the top of the page.

However, shots can end at the bottom of a page. When they do, the following page begins with a new slug, not a CONTINUED.

The guideline for the use of CONTINUED at the bottom of the page is similar to the rule for the top of the page. If you begin the top of a page with a slug (indicating that the shot has ended at the bottom of the preceding page), you *do not* write CONTINUED at the bottom of the preceding page. If the top of the page begins with CONTINUED, then the bottom of the preceding page also contains a CONTINUED, indicating that the shot is ongoing.

Now you know how to use CONTINUED. However, as you have seen from the examples, the CONTINUED at the top of the page differs somewhat in form from the CONTINUED at the bottom of the page.

The CONTINUED at the page's top is written in all caps and followed by a colon—

CONTINUED:

The top-of-the-page CONTINUED begins at horizontal space fourteen and is placed approximately one inch from the top edge of the paper.

The CONTINUED at the page's bottom is written in caps and enclosed by parentheses.

(CONTINUED)

The bottom-of-the-page CONTINUED begins at space sixty-one, as do cuts, and is double-spaced down from the final direction or dialogue on the page. Because a slug can never be orphaned, the bottom CONTINUED never immediately follows a slug. There must be intervening direction or dialogue or the slug must be moved to the next page.

Some writers have stopped using CONTINUED altogether; some others use it incorrectly.

Use of the CONTINUED remains a courtesy to a reader because it lets him or her know that the shot is ongoing. It also shows that the writer knows standard script format.

A REVIEW OF THE RULES FOR MARGINALS

The title:

1) appears on the first page of the screenplay only.
2) begins six lines—about one and one-eighth inches—from the top edge of the paper.
3) is in all caps.
4) is centered.
5) is enclosed in quotation marks.

THE END:

1) appears on the last page of your screenplay only.
2) is placed six lines below FADE OUT.
3) is in all caps.
4) is centered.
5) is underlined.

The page number:

1) appears on every page but the first.
2) is written four to six lines from the top edge of the paper.
3) begins 7.3 inches from the left edge of the paper, or at space seventy-three.
4) may be written in one of three ways:
   a) 73
   b) 73.
   c) -73-
   In the last case, place the first hyphen at space seventy-two.

Top-of-the-page CONTINUED:

1) is in all caps.
2) is followed by a colon.
3) begins at space fourteen.
4) is placed approximately one inch from the top of the paper.
5) is not used if the page begins with a slug.

Bottom-of-the-page CONTINUED:

1) is in all caps.
2) enclosed in parentheses.
3) begins at space sixty-one (as do the cuts and FADE OUT.).
4) is double-spaced from the final direction or dialogue on the page.
5) never follows a slug unless direction or dialogue intervenes.
6) is not used if a CUT TO: is the last item on the page.
7) is not used if the following page begins with a slug.

In the following exercise taken from Betty Blackburn's "Strangers in This World," the first five-page version has several errors in the use of marginals. Go through these pages and edit the marginals using the guidelines you have just learned. Then compare your corrections to the corrected pages that follow. An asterisk (*) indicates where a correction has been made.

JACK

still stares at Lige, a look of unbelieving awe on his face. Jack grabs the snake box and hurries out the back of the church with it.

THE SHERIFF AND POSSE

burst into the back of the church.

MEETING ROOM

The sheriff runs down the middle aisle. The others fan out.

> SHERIFF
> Take 'em with the snakes on 'em,
> boys.

He hauls up short at the dais: looks around.

Two members of the posse and Callahan look under benches, behind the lectern, in the anteroom.

Jack reenters by the front door.

The sheriff looks up, sees Jack, yells.

> SHERIFF
> What the hell are you doing here?
> What become of those snakes.

Jack laughs.

> JACK
> What kind of liquor you been
> drinking, Sheriff?

The sheriff marches up the aisle.

JACK AND THE SHERIFF

The sheriff takes Jack by the arm and starts up the aisle with him.

> SHERIFF
> I got this straight. I'll make a
> witness outta you.

The choir breaks forth with "I AM A STRANGER IN THIS WORLD" o.s., continues till the sheriff leaves.

(CONTINUED)

JACK AND THE SHERIFF

The sheriff has Jack by the arm.

> JACK
> You arresting me, Sheriff?

The sheriff releases Jack with a disgusted shove.

> SHERIFF
> I'll see your city editor. Conspiring
> with these heathens.

THE SHERIFF

motions his deputies.

> SHERIFF
> C' mon, fellows.

MEETING ROOM

The still-singing, stunned congregation watches the door where the
posse departed. Lige leaves the dais and goes up the aisle to Jack, puts
an arm on his shoulder and leads him down the aisle.

> LIGE
> Thank you, brother.

Members of the congregation crowd around Jack, embrace him.

JACK

looks at them, bewildered. Around him the clapping, shouting starts
with a vengeance.

MEETING ROOM

The snake box reappears on the dais.

The shouting and dancing quickly moves into a rhapsodic stage.

Members dance the "jerks," babble.

(CONTINUED)

LIGE

at the lectern, cries out over the hubbub.

> LIGE
> God is with us tonight, folks. The
> Holy Ghost is here amongst us.
> Here to uphold my hands. Yes, the
> Holy Ghost...

He goes off into the "jerks," speaks in tongues, crosses over and kicks the snake box, swoops down, opens it and snatches out the rattler. O.s. the shouting, CLAPPING becomes louder.

Lige holds the snake aloft, parades the length of the church.

Some members draw away from him, some draw toward the upheld snake in a writhing pattern.

MEETING ROOM

Lige returns to the dais, gives the snake to first one and then another of the members, who have seizures and approach him. He takes the snake back.

LIGE

moves toward Virgie, who dances in her own hypnosis.

VIRGIE

sees Lige and the snake and freezes in fright as he comes closer. She shakes from head to foot and calls out frantically.

> VIRGIE
> Oh, Lige...

Then in an automatic voice,

> VIRGIE
> (continuing)
> ...Lord, save us.

Lige extends the snake above her head.

(CONTINUED)

116

JACK

is stricken, lifts a hand to interfere.

JACK'S POV

Virgie goes into a trance. Her unfocused eyes close.

JACK

is disconcerted, draws back, eyes averted.

VIRGIE

stands immobile, hardly breathes, as Lige's hands wind the snake around her head, as a coronet.

JACK

turns toward a dark window, sees his disheveled reflection, closes his eyes.

MINNIE

brings forth another snake: another appears beside her in another dancer's hands: then another behind her.

Minnie glides smoothly with the snake toward the front of the church.

JACK

stands at the window, eyes closed, as arms, legs, snakes swirl haphazardly around him. The singing, CLAPPING o.s. reaches a crescendo.

Jack opens his eyes. Reflected in the window Virgie's head, still and surreal, with the undulating coronet.

Jack turns slowly and stares at Virgie, motionless.

JACK'S POV

Minnie moves between Jack and Virgie, dances provocatively with a snake. The snake's head weaves toward a sleeping baby in its mother arms.

(CONTINUED)

JACK

panics, rushes out of the church.

INT. MEETING ROOM - LATER THAT NIGHT

Lige sits on a bench at the front of the dimly lit empty meeting room.
Virgie kneels in front of him. He puts a hand on her head.

> LIGE
> I'm an old men, Virgie, but I'm
> still a man. I kin offer ye a
> partnership of the spirit.

> VIRGIE
> I ain't fitten.

> LIGE
> Ain't any of us fitten.

He kneels beside her. He takes her hand; they gaze into each other's
eyes.

JACK

still stares at Lige, a look of unbelieving awe on his face. Jack grabs the snake box and hurries out the back of the church with it.

THE SHERIFF AND POSSE

burst into the back of the church.

MEETING ROOM

The sheriff runs down the middle aisle. The others fan out.

> SHERIFF
> Take 'em with the snakes on 'em,
> boys.

He hauls up short at the dais: looks around.

Two members of the posse and Callahan look under benches, behind the lectern, in the anteroom.

Jack reenters by the front door.

The sheriff looks up, sees Jack, yells.

> SHERIFF
> What the hell are you doing here?
> What become of those snakes.

Jack laughs.

> JACK
> What kind of liquor you been
> drinking, Sheriff?

The sheriff marches up the aisle.

JACK AND THE SHERIFF

The sheriff takes Jack by the arm and starts up the aisle with him.

> SHERIFF
> I got this straight. I'll make a
> witness outta you.

The choir breaks forth with "I AM A STRANGER IN THIS WORLD" O.S., continues till the sheriff leaves.*

*

JACK AND THE SHERIFF

The sheriff has Jack by the arm.

                    JACK
          You arresting me, Sheriff?

The sheriff releases Jack with a disgusted shove.

                   SHERIFF
          I'll see your city editor. Conspiring
          with these heathens.

THE SHERIFF

motions his deputies.

                   SHERIFF
          C'mon, fellows.

MEETING ROOM
The still-singing, stunned congregation watches the door where the
posse departed. Lige leaves the dais and goes up the aisle to Jack, puts
an arm on his shoulder and leads him down the aisle.

                    LIGE
          Thank you, brother.

Members of the congregation crowd around Jack, embrace him.

JACK

looks at them, bewildered. Around him the clapping, shouting starts
with a vengeance.

MEETING ROOM

The snake box reappears on the dais.

The shouting and dancing quickly moves into a rhapsodic stage.

Members dance the "jerks," babble.*
*

120

*

LIGE

at the lectern, cries out over the hubbub.

> LIGE
> God is with us tonight, folks. The
> Holy Ghost is here amongst us.
> Here to uphold my hands. Yes, the
> Holy Ghost...

He goes off into the "jerks," speaks in tongues, crosses over and kicks the snake box, swoops down, opens it and snatches out the rattler. O.s. the shouting, CLAPPING becomes louder.

Lige holds the snake aloft, parades the length of the church.

Some members draw away from him, some draw toward the upheld snake in a writhing pattern.

MEETING ROOM

Lige returns to the dais, gives the snake to first one and then another of the members, who have seizures and approach him. He takes the snake back.

LIGE

moves toward Virgie, who dances in her own hypnosis.

VIRGIE

sees Lige and the snake and freezes in fright as he comes closer. She shakes from head to foot and calls out frantically.

> VIRGIE
> Oh, Lige...

Then in an automatic voice,

> VIRGIE
> (continuing)
> ...Lord, save us.

Lige extends the snake above her head.
*

*

JACK

is stricken, lifts a hand to interfere.

JACK'S POV

Virgie goes into a trance. Her unfocused eyes close.

JACK

is disconcerted, draws back, eyes averted.

VIRGIE

stands immobile, hardly breathes, as Lige's hands wind the snake around her head, as a coronet.

JACK

turns toward a dark window, sees his disheveled reflection, closes his eyes.

MINNIE

brings forth another snake: another appears beside her in another dancer's hands: then another behind her.

Minnie glides smoothly with the snake toward the front of the church.

JACK

stands at the window, eyes closed, as arms, legs, snakes swirl haphazardly around him. The singing, CLAPPING o.s. reaches a crescendo.

Jack opens his eyes. Reflected in the window Virgie's head, still and surreal, with the undulating coronet.

Jack turns slowly and stares at Virgie, motionless.

JACK'S POV

Minnie moves between Jack and Virgie, dances provocatively with a snake. The snake's head weaves toward a sleeping baby in its mother's arms.
*

*
JACK

panics, rushes out of the church.

INT. MEETING ROOM - LATER THAT NIGHT

Lige sits on a bench at the front of the dimly lit empty meeting room. Virgie kneels in front of him. He puts a hand on her head.

                    LIGE
          I'm an old men, Virgie, but I'm
          still a man. I kin offer ye a
          partnership of the spirit.

                    VIRGIE
          I ain't fitten.

                    LIGE
          Ain't any of us fitten.

He kneels beside her. He takes her hand; they gaze into each other's eyes.

CHAPTER
10

Review of Spacing Rules

We have covered separately the five essential elements of screenplay format and their proper spacing. For a convenient reference, let's put the spacing rules together.

The five elements are:
1. Slugs
2. Directions
3. Dialogue
4. Fades and cuts
5. Marginals

A REVIEW OF RULES FOR HORIZONTAL SPACING

1) All slugs, directions, FADE IN:, and the top-of-the-page CONTINUED: begin 1.4 inches from the left edge of the paper, or at space fourteen.
2) In dialogue:
   a) the character cue begins 4.1 inches from the left edge of the paper, or at space forty-one.
   b) the speech begins 2.8 inches from the left edge of the paper, or at space twenty-eight.
   c) the parenthetical, enclosed by parentheses, begins 3.5 inches from the left edge of the paper, or at space thirty-five.

3) The two cuts (CUT TO: AND MATCH CUT:), the bottom-of-the-page (CONTINUED), and FADE OUT. begin at 6.1 inches from the left edge of the paper, or at space sixty-one.

4) The page number begins 7.3 inches from the left edge of the paper, or at space seventy-three. If you place hyphens on either side of the number (-23-), the first hyphen is placed at space seventy-two. On the first page of the script, the page number is omitted.

5) The title on the first page and <u>THE END</u> on the last page are always centered horizontally.

A REVIEW OF THE RULES FOR VERTICAL SPACING

1) Whether your shot ends with direction, dialogue, or a cut, always triple-space to the following slug. (The sole exception is the first slug in your screenplay, which is double-spaced down from the FADE IN:.)

2) Double-space from a slug to the following direction or dialogue.

3) Single-space within a:
   a) paragraph of direction.
   b) paragraph of dialogue.

4) Double-space between:
   a) the top of the page CONTINUED: and the direction or dialogue that follows.
   b) paragraphs of direction.
   c) paragraphs of direction and dialogue.
   d) direction and a cut.
   e) direction and a bottom-of-the-page (CONTINUED).
   f) paragraphs of dialogue.
   g) dialogue and a cut.
   h) dialogue and a bottom-of-the-page (CONTINUED).
   i) FADE IN: and the first slug.
   j) The final direction or dialogue in the screenplay and FADE OUT.

5) Triple-space from the title to FADE IN: on page one.

6) Place the title on page one, six lines from the top of the paper.

7) Place <u>THE END</u> six lines below FADE OUT. (If there is not enough room on your page, not to worry. By the time the reader gets to <u>THE END</u>, he or she is not going to chuck your screenplay because <u>THE END</u> is only two or three spaces below FADE OUT.)

In part one of the following exercise, taken from Jim Helm's "Managua," I have inserted several errors in the use of spacing. Go through these pages and edit them using the guidelines you have just learned. Then in part two compare your corrections with the same scene presented correctly as the author wrote it. An asterisk indicates where corrections have been made.

EXT. HOTEL/PARKING LOT - DAY

A soldier inside Stoney's van calls to Miguel.

BESIDE VAN

The paneling from inside Stoney's van has been removed.
    A soldier squats in the doorway.

He shows Miguel his finger covered with gun grease.

Miguel rubs the grease between his fingers and looks toward the hotel.

      INT. HOTEL/OUTSIDE STONEY'S DOOR

Stoney opens the door to his room, looks down the hallway.

HALLWAY

Stoney steps out of his room, walks to the next door and unlocks it. He
glances down the hallway toward the elevator, steps in the room and
closes the door.

ELEVATOR

door opens and Miguel walks down the hallway toward Stoney's room.
He takes a .45 pistol from its holster.

Miguel pauses at Stoney's door, cocks the weapon. He knocks on the
door.

                MIGUEL
      Señor Jackson?

Miguel takes a passkey from his pocket and unlocks the door. He
pushes the door open with his foot and goes in waving his pistol.

CUT TO:

STONEY'S ROOM
Stoney rushes through the doorway and crashes into Miguel. Miguel
raises the .45 and tries to turn around as Stoney grabs him from
behind.

                      CONTINUED:

They fall to the floor, Stoney grabs Miguel's hand and twists the pistol loose. Stoney puts the pistol to Miguel's head.

STONEY AND MIGUEL

> STONEY
> You have my passport, amigo.

Stoney stands and pulls Miguel to his feet. He kicks the door shut with his foot.

Miguel nurses his bruised trigger finger.

> MIGUEL
> You... make mistake.

> STONEY
> You made the mistake. One
> question. How do I find the
> Sandinistas without getting my
> ass shot off?

frightened

> MIGUEL
> The... Cali next to Lake Managua

leads to the barrios where

Edwardo's soldiers are, but...

> STONEY
> You're taking me there.

> MIGUEL
> Señor, you are loco.

> STONEY
> I can't argue with you about that.

EXT. HOTEL/PARKING LOT - DAY

A soldier inside Stoney's van calls to Miguel.

BESIDE VAN

*The paneling from inside Stoney's van has been removed.

*A soldier squats in the doorway.

*He shows Miguel his finger covered with gun grease.

Miguel rubs the grease between his fingers and looks toward the hotel.

*INT. HOTEL/OUTSIDE STONEY'S DOOR

Stoney opens the door to his room, looks down the hallway.

HALLWAY

Stoney steps out of his room, walks to the next door and unlocks it. He glances down the hallway toward the elevator, steps in the room and closes the door.

ELEVATOR

door opens and Miguel walks down the hallway toward Stoney's room. He takes a .45 pistol from its holster.

Miguel pauses at Stoney's door, cocks the weapon. He knocks on the door.

> MIGUEL
> Señor Jackson?

Miguel takes a passkey from his pocket and unlocks the door. He pushes the door open with his foot and goes in waving his pistol.*

STONEY'S ROOM

*Stoney rushes through the doorway and crashes into Miguel. Miguel raises the .45 and tries to turn around as Stoney grabs him from behind.

They fall to the floor, Stoney grabs Miguel's hand and twists the pistol loose. Stoney puts the pistol to Miguel's head.

STONEY AND MIGUEL

                    *STONEY
          You have my passport, amigo.

Stoney stands and pulls Miguel to his feet. He kicks the door shut with
his foot.

Miguel nurses his bruised trigger finger.

                    *MIGUEL
          You... make mistake.

                    STONEY
          *You made the mistake. One
          question. How do I find the
          Sandinistas without getting my
          ass shot off?

frightened

                    MIGUEL
          *The... Cali next to Lake Managua
          leads to the barrios where
          Edwardo's soldiers are, but...

                    STONEY
          You're taking me there.

                    MIGUEL
          Señor, you are loco.

                    STONEY
          I can't argue with you about that.

HOTEL LOBBY/ELEVATOR

The elevator door opens and Stoney and Miguel walk through the
lobby toward the hotel entrance. Stoney has his hand in the pocket
of his jacket.

                                                        CUT TO:

EXT. SANDINISTA STRONGHOLD - LATER

In front of the ruins of a bank building, sandbags are stacked shoulder
high. Sandinista soldiers fire over the sandbags at the building across
the street.

BEHIND SANDBAGS

GENERAL EDUARDO PASTORIA stands in front of the blown-out windows of the bank. Beside him a soldier carries the radio on his back from which Eduardo is talking.

They speak in Spanish.

EDUARDO AND SOLDIER

> EDUARDO
> No, return to the banco. What?

Eduardo shakes his head and hands the soldier the phone.

> SOLDIER
> Platoon is in trouble, General?

> EDUARDO
> No, something about a blue
> autobús in the area.

CALI CENTRAL BOULEVARD

The four-lane boulevard is littered with dead soldiers and burning vehicles.

Stoney's van speeds down the corner of the street.

INSIDE VAN

Miguel drives and Stoney sits in the passenger's seat holding the .45 pistol on Miguel.

O.s. heavy gunfire.

Frightened.

> MIGUEL
> Ahead is road block.

Points pistol at Miguel's head.

> STONEY
> Run it!

130

CALI CENTRAL BOULEVARD

Four soldiers behind wooden sawhorses watch Stoney's van speed towards them. Jeeps sit on both sides of the sawhorses. Three soldiers run behind the jeeps, but one soldier stays behind shouting for the van to stop.

The soldier aims his rifle at Stoney's van... then runs out of the way as the van crashes through the sawhorses and speeds down the street.

The soldiers fire at the van as it rounds a corner at the end of the street.

INSIDE VAN

Screams.

> MIGUEL
> Chinga a tu madre.

> STONEY
> Get back on the main street.

SIDE STREET

Miguel swings the van around in the middle of the street, barely misses a burning car. The rear of the van clips the side of a building as it heads back toward Cali Central.

INSIDE VAN

O.s. pieces of brick hit the top of the van.

Laughs.

> STONEY
> You may have just bought yourself
> a building, amigo. Come on, move
> it!

Miguel glances at the .45 in Stoney's hand and floors the van.

CALI CENTRAL BOULEVARD

Miguel speeds the van down the street. At the end of the street sits the bank building surrounded by sandbags. Heavy fighting erupts from the bank and building across the street.

INSIDE VAN

Miguel shakes his head.

> MIGUEL
> Ahead is Sandinistas. We go no
> further.

> STONEY
> Keep driving!

EXT. CALI CENTRAL BOULEVARD

The van speeds down the center of the street.

WIDER VIEW

Heavy fire from the bank building and the smaller building
across the street.

TOP OF SMALLER BUILDING

A Somoza soldier aims his rifle at the moving van.

INSIDE VAN

Miguel's windshield shatters and he screams as the bullet hits him in
the chest.

EXT. CALI CENTRAL BOULEVARD

The van swerves to the left and slows down as it hits the side of a
building half a block from the bank.

VAN

The side passenger window shatters. Stoney opens the door and rolls
out onto the pavement. Miguel is slumped across the steering wheel.

WIDER VIEW

The snipers' bullets splatter pavement around Stoney. He scrambles
toward an alley next to the van.

ALLEY

Stoney runs between the two buildings. He sees a dead soldier next to an overturned garbage can. Stoney slows to a walk.

Stoney looks back down the alley toward the van.

STONEY'S POV

A jeep with four Somoza soldiers speeds down the alley toward him.

BACK TO SCENE

Stoney runs down the alley.

The driver shifts gears. A soldier standing in the back of the jeep behind a .50 caliber machine gun cocks the weapon.

OPEN FIELD

Behind the building sits an abandoned baseball diamond. A hundred yards away is the side of the bank building.

Stoney runs from the alley into the open field toward the side entrance of the bank. The jeep ROARS in hot pursuit.

SIDE DOOR OF BANK

opens and two Sandinista soldiers with automatic rifles run toward Stoney and the jeep.

OPEN FIELD

The driver closes the distance between the jeep and Stoney. The soldier in the jeep swings the machine gun towards the Sandinistas.

Bullets tear across the soldier's chest as the jeep swerves toward Stoney.

Stoney sees the Sandinistas firing at the jeep. Stoney runs backwards also firing at the jeep.

JEEP

The driver is hit in the throat, falls forward over the steering wheel.

(CONTINUED)

The jeep skids into Stoney, its left fender strikes a glancing blow that throws him to the ground.

WIDER VIEW

Stoney hits the ground on his back as the jeep turns over, throwing the soldiers in the air like rag dolls.

The Sandinistas run toward the jeep firing at the soldiers scrambling to their feet.

Stoney lays on his back moaning. The gunfire stops.

STONEY'S POV

Two Sandinistas stand over him. They grin broadly.

BACK TO SCENE

Stoney raises a limp hand and points his trigger finger at the Sandinistas.

Whispers.

>STONEY
>Bang... bang.

Stoney drops his hand to the ground and passes out.

                                                        CUT TO:

Part Three

ALL DRESSED UP WITH SOMEPLACE TO GO

CHAPTER
11

Dressing Your Script
(So It Can Be Seen in Public)

What are you going to wear the night you accept your Oscar? I predict that it won't be torn jeans and a T-shirt that says, "THEY DON'T CALL ME GOOD FOR NOTHING."

Just as there are dress codes for social occasions, there is a dress code for filmscripts. A properly dressed script has a title page and is bound in a specific fashion.

Place the *title page* before page one of your script. On the title page you place the *title,* the name(s) of the *author(s), company name* if applicable, *address,* and *phone number.* If you adapted the screenplay from another work, you should indicate the title and the form of that work and the author: 'STRANGERS IN THIS WORLD,' adapted from a play of the same title by Brainard Chaney." On some screenplays you may need to indicate who created the story. The title page does *not* include a copyright notice ©, a Registered WGA notice and/or the WGA number, a date, or any indication of which screenplay draft you have submitted.

The following page is an example of a title page.

"FIVE AND DIME KIDS"

Written by

Rick Reichman

PO BOX 2592
Merrifield, VA 22116-2592
(703) 555-0568

138

On the title page, begin your title at approximately four inches, or seventeen lines, from the top of the page. The title is centered, written in all caps, enclosed in quotation marks. It is not underlined as it has not yet been published or produced.

After the title, triple-space, center, and write "Written by." The *W* is capped, the rest is lower-case. You may wonder why you need the words written by when it seems obvious that the name(s) following the title indicates the writer(s). But, as noted above, you may also need "Story by" or "Adapted from" on the title page. So it is best to be absolutely clear about who did what for the screenplay.

Double-space from "Written by" and write in your name or your name and the name of your partner (co-author). Names are centered. If there is more than one, place an ampersand (&) between them to indicate partners.

Author's Name & Partner's Name

If you and your co-author are equal partners in the writing of the script, always use the ampersand, and not the spelled-out word "and."

The word "and" between writers' names usually indicates that the second writer rewrote the script. (This frequently happens after the first writer sells the screenplay.)

If the screenplay needs a "Story by" or "Adapted from," triple-space down from the author's name and place the capital *S* or *A* at 1.4 inches from the left edge, or space fourteen. Then you may finish in one of two ways.

After the "from" or "by," move two horizontal spaces and provide the necessary information. Alternatively, triple-space down and begin the necessary information beneath the "from" or "by."

After you have completed the above information, go approximately three-quarters of the way down the page, or to line thirty-nine. On either the right or left-hand side of the title page, place the name of your company (if you have a company), your address, and your phone number. The company name, address, and phone number should be one paragraph, single-spaced. If you place this information on the right-hand side, the end of the longest line should be flush with the right margin.

The page should include nothing else. Anything else on the title page is clutter and immediately shouts "amateur."

Binding Your Script

Binding is as important to the look of the script as the script pages themselves. Why spend time learning format only to send out your script bound like a high school English assignment? As a recent ad campaign goes, you get only one chance to make a first impression.

Scripts are bound simply. The script has front and back covers, has three holes punched in the standard pattern—a top hole approximately 1.5 inches down the page, a hole in the middle at 5.5 inches down the page, and a bottom hole approximately 9.75 inches down the page—and is bound with two brass, round-headed fasteners, usually two inches long.

Script covers are 110-pound, 8½-by-11-inch card stock, any color but white. It is cheapest to buy the card stock in reams at an office or paper supply store or print shop. Some companies consider a ream of card stock to be 500 sheets, others 250 sheets.

Two-hundred-fifty or especially 500 covers may seem more than you will ever use. However, with all the script copies you will make and with all the covers you will replace, the card stock disappears quickly.

As for getting your paper and card stock in three-hole punched, I suggest two approaches. Find a friendly local printer or perhaps even a small publisher, who has a drill. He or she can three-hole punch reams at a time. This job should be done for a dollar or so. In addition, buy a reasonably good quality, standard three hole-punch for home use.

Brass, round-headed fasteners can usually be found at a business stationary store, business supply store, or sometimes a college book store. The fasteners come in boxes of 100. From the head extend two prongs, one pointed at the end, the other rounded. The pointed prong is slightly longer.

Round-headed fasteners come in several lengths. For most screenplays between 90 and 120 pages in length, the two-inch size—labeled number 7—is best.

Before fastening your script, make sure the script pages are in order. Then insert fasteners in the top and bottom holes of the script. Leave the middle hole empty.

Separate the prongs and flatten each against the back of the script. Then take each of the prongs and bend the end-half back toward the center. The fastener will form a bow-tie shape. This keeps the prongs from appearing too long, and from catching on and/or wounding other scripts, papers, clothes, surrounding objects, or reader.

Prices for paper, covers, hole punching, and fasteners vary considerably. It pays to shop around.

Do not write on the covers or on the side of the script. Make sure that the covers and page edges are clean and blank.

Now you are ready to send your script.

A Review of the Rules for Dressing Your Script

On the title page:

1) Begin the title at approximately four inches, or seventeen lines, from the top of the page.
2) Center the title.
3) Write the title in all caps.
4) Enclose the title in quotation marks.
5) Triple-space from the title and write the words "Written by."
6) "Written by" should be centered.

7) "Written by" begins with a capital *W*. The rest is in lower-case type.

8) Double-space from "Written by" and write the name(s) of the author(s).

9) The name(s) should be centered.

10) The name(s) should be written in upper-and lower-case letters.

11) Use an ampersand between names of partners.

12) For "Story by" or "Adapted from," triple-space down from the name(s) of the author(s).

13) Begin "Story by" or "Adapted from" at space fourteen.

14) Finish "Story by" or "Adapted from" by moving three spaces on the same line and adding the necessary information or by triple-spacing and beginning the necessary information under the by or from.

15) Approximately three-fourths of the way down the page, or on line thirty-nine, write, in a single-spaced paragraph, company name if applicable, then your address and telephone number.

The script:

1) has front and back covers of 110-pound, 8½-by-11-inch-inch card stock, any color but white.

2) has covers, title page, and standard three hole punch.

3) is bound by two number 7 brass, round-headed fasteners in the top and bottom holes.

4) has no writing on the covers or the edges.

In part one of the following exercise, taken from Allan Moyé's "A Place to Die," I have inserted several errors in the title page. Go through these pages and edit them using the guidelines you have just learned. Then in part two compare your corrections with the same scene presented correctly as the author wrote it. An asterisk indicates where corrections have been made.

A Place to Die

By:

Allan Moyé

ADDRESS

Milltown, VA 20710

703-555-1991

WGA Registered 27561

Fourth Draft

July 27, 1989

(C) 1989

142

"A PLACE TO DIE"

Written by

Allan Moyé

ADDRESS
Milltown, VA 20710
(703) 555-1991

CHAPTER
12

The Right "Look" for
a Filmscript

"THE LOOK!"

The look is numero uno when readers, agents, producers, and others first assess your work. The look is what initially separates the pop from the corn, the milk from the duds. So what is the look?

When a reader, agent, producer, or most any other industry professional first sees your screenplay, she or he gives it three quick tests. Are the cover and binding correct? Is the number of script pages appropriate—105 to 115 pages, never exceeding 120 or dropping below ninety? Do your pages have the look? That is—are your pages easy-to-read, formatted properly, and balanced almost 50/50 between ink and white space? If your screenplay passes these tests, it signals that you have probably written a professional, producable script.

You should pass the first two tests easily. Passing test three is easier to write about than to do. But there are some easy DOs and DON'Ts that can help.

DO use:
      short paragraphs
      pithy speeches
      correct format

DON'T use:

>
> detailed slugs
>
> long, descriptive paragraphs
>
> many long speeches

Also, be sure not to repeat what you have already stated. It is surprising to see how many scripts contain ideas or actions described three or four times with only slight variation in the wording.

There are two page looks that some screenwriting teachers advise against, the "flag page" and the "T" page. The flag page alternates a line or two of direction and a line or two of dialogue all the way down the page. The following page is an example of a flag page.

Russ leans against the wall as he talks on the phone.

                    RUSS
          It's my company, my operation.

Russ impatiently paces the area around the phone.

                    RUSS
          I didn't say anything about going
          to the hospital...

He shakes his head.

                    RUSS
                 (continuing)
          Operation... I was talking about my
          business.

Now he rolls eyes and looks at the ceiling.

                    RUSS
          No, not none of your business. I
          asked the bank about a loan.

Now he cups his face in his hands and shakes his head.

                    RUSS
          I am not alone. Sally's just gone
          for a bit on vacation.

He rolls his eyes again and laughs.

                    RUSS
          She didn't get bit. I said she was
          gone for a while.

He puts the receiver down and walks the circumference of the room.
He picks up the receiver, listens, and answers.

                    RUSS
          What do you mean, you thought
          she was gone from the beginning?

He listens intently.

                    RUSS
          That was little Miss Tiff. She
          wasn't exactly the girl-next-door.

He presses his hands together, cracking some knuckles.

                    RUSS
          I realize she just lived across the
          street. What I meant was...

Avoid flag pages because they signal automatically that the page is filled with nonessential business for the actors. The page both looks like—and raises—a flag. There are better ways to present your story.

The T page begins or ends with a directional paragraph, but the rest of the page contains only dialogue. This pattern forms a large T, either right-side up or inverted, on the page. The following page is an example of a T page.

Russ paces impatiently as he talks on the phone. He stops, shakes his head, and paces again. Finally, he picks up a deck of cards and tosses them, one by one, at a small basketball goal nearby.

> RUSS
> It's my company, my operation.

> RUSS
> I didn't say anything about going to the hospital...

> RUSS
> (continuing)
> Operation... for crying out loud, I was talking about my business.

> RUSS
> No, not none of your business. I asked the bank about a loan.

> RUSS
> I am not alone. Sally's just gone for a bit on vacation.

> RUSS
> She didn't get bit. I said she was gone for a while.

> RUSS
> What do you mean, you thought she was gone from the beginning?

> RUSS
> That was little Miss Tiff. She wasn't exactly the girl-next-door.

> RUSS
> I know she just lived across the street. What I meant was...

> RUSS
> How can you say that?

> RUSS
> Isn't that how fish and people get in trouble? Opening their big mouths.

> RUSS
> Not big moths. We don't have any moths...

Some find the T page awkward and unbalanced, so it is best to avoid it if you can.

If dialogue is used as sparingly as possible, if direction is in short, well-written paragraphs, and if your cuts and fades and marginals are placed correctly, then the pages you write should definitely create that look of success.

In part one of the following exercise, taken from Ralph Nurnberger's & Susan Tieger's "Co-op," I have inserted several errors in the use of the look. Go through these pages and edit them using the guidelines you have just learned. Then in part two compare your corrections with the same scene presented correctly as the author wrote it. An asterisk indicates where corrections have been made.

APARTMENT - LATER

David sits at the table in the living room studying the Yellow Pages.
The buzzer RINGS, the dogs next door BARK. David goes down the
long, dark corridor to the door.

DOORWAY

David has to almost pick up the police lock and set it in its open
position. Twice the bar slips and clunks onto the floor. The third time
he watches intently as the lock seems to slide, jump, move, and finally
settle as it should.

David opens the door. He is surprised by two medics, who rush past
him into the apartment.

APARTMENT

The FIRST MEDIC is young, white, and has a day-old beard. He is
dressed in a dark colored T-shirt and a white jacket. The SECOND
MEDIC man is black and wears regular medic dress.

                    MEDIC 1
          Where's the patient?

                    DAVID
          She's not a patient. She's dead.

                    MEDIC 2
          Then why the hell did you call an
          ambulance? We're busy enough
          without prank calls.

                    DAVID
          I... I called for a coroner.

Both medics exchange glances.

                    MEDIC 1
          Gladys!

Medic 2 nods and goes to the phone to place a call. Medic 1 runs his
hand through his hair, then sticks his hands into his pockets as he
surveys the place.

MEDIC 1 AND DAVID

> MEDIC 1
> Anyone else beside the dead lady
> live here?

> DAVID
> No, she really valued her privacy.

> MEDIC 1
> Hey, pal, this pad could be great.
> You got any plans to sublet?

DAVID'S POV

Plaster hangs from the ten-foot-high ceilings. The crown-molding has separated from the walls in several places. Soot, dust, and dirt streak the walls. Parquet floor squares are missing.

David shakes his head.

APARTMENT

Medic 2 finishes the call and both prepare to leave.

> MEDIC 2
> The police will be here soon. I'd
> suggest you find a funeral home.

Medic 1 writes his name and phone number on a sheet of paper, rips it from his notebook, and hands it to David.

> MEDIC 1
> Give me a call if you want to
> sublease this apartment.

They open the door and leave.

DAVID

goes to the telephone.

DAVID'S CONVERSATION

David is already in the midst of the dialogue.

(CONTINUED)

                              DAVID
                    ... ten thousand dollars just to pick
                    her up and bury her? I don't need
                    a gold-lined casket and the
                    Mormon Tabernacle Choir.

                              DAVID
                    All I need is a simple... That is the
                    price for your simple burial?

                              DAVID
                    No, damn it, I don't know what I'm
                    going to do with her apartment.

David slams down the receiver. Bell RINGS, dogs next door BARK.

DAVID

arrives at the door, fumbles with the locks. The police lock moves only
slightly better this time, as David has it slip only once. Finally, David
opens the door.

DOORWAY

two uniformed POLICEMEN wait in the hallway.

Officer BILL O'BRIEN, in his fifties, and TONY D'ANGELO, in his late
twenties, carry coffee and a box of donuts.

APARTMENT

Bill and Tony sit at the table. David answers their questions as he
takes inventory of the apartment.

TWO POLICEMEN AND DAVID

                              BILL
                    You live here?

                              DAVID
                    I'm a chemistry teacher in
                    Virginia.

                              TONY
                    If you don't live here, the
                    apartment will have to be sealed
                    for about a week while we conduct
                    a thorough investigation.
                                                        (CONTINUED)

> BILL
> Course if you lived here, then you
> can stay, and we don't have to
> investigate. Saves a lot of
> paperwork.

Tony turns to his partner.

> TONY
> Bill, ask him the question again.

> BILL
> Do you live here?

> DAVID
> Whenever I'm in New York.

They both grin and nod.

> TONY
> Good enough. Any other relatives?

> DAVID
> No. I'm her only living relative.

> TONY
> That makes it yours... sort of.

As they write, David enters the kitchen.

When David returns a moment later, he carries an old tin box. He
comes to the table.

TABLE AREA

He places the tin on the table.

> DAVID
> My aunt's. She probably baked
> them yesterday. God, she made
> great cookies.

Everyone digs in.

> BILL
> They're even better than my
> donuts.

> BILL
> We still need a coroner to fill out
> the death certificate.

(CONTINUED)

                              TONY
          If you're serious about going back
          to Virginia, I'd love to sublease
          this apartment from you. I'm not
          sure it's legal. But that's okay,
          I'm a cop.

                              DAVID
          I'm still not sure what...

The doorbell RINGS. The dogs in 5B BARK.

                              BILL
          Good, the coroner.

HALLWAY

BERNICE BAUMGARTNER, a dumpy woman in her fifties, wearing a
name tag, holds a covered tray, is already speaking.

                              BERNICE
          Hello, Miss Richards. We brought
          your dinner. This evening, we
          have roast chic...

The door opens.

BERNICE AND DAVID

                              BERNICE
          Oh, my, you're not Miss Richards.

                              DAVID
          No, she passed away last night.

                              BERNICE
          Oh, I'm so sorry. Such a lovely old
          lady. We at Meals on Wheels loved
          bringing her food every day.

                              DAVID
          And I know she appreciated it. She
          told...

                              BERNICE
          We were such good friends. I know
          that she would want me to
          continue to look after her place.

                              DAVID
          Pardon me?

                                              (CONTINUED)

154

                    BERNICE
          Oh, my, you wouldn't know, not
          being here, but I know she would
          have liked to have my daughter
          sublet her place. Being rent
          controlled and...

                    DAVID
          Your daughter...?

                    BERNICE
          ... You'd like my daughter. Are you
          Jewish? Are you single? Are you
          straight? In today's world... You
          know.

                    DAVID
          No, I really don't know.

David shuts the door. But just as it closes, the bell RINGS again.
Frustrated, David opens the door.

DOORWAY

The CORONER steps inside. He looks like Rosy Grier and dresses like
Sherlock Holmes. He even smokes a Cavendish pipe.

                    DAVID
          Coroner?

The man nods.

DINING ROOM

The police sit at the table eating.

BEDROOM

David watches the coroner as he pulls the sheet back over her body.

                    CORONER
          You're right, she's dead.

Coroner takes out clipboard and writes on the form.

                    CORONER
Heart attack.

                                                        (CONTINUED)

                                                              155

                    DAVID
          Excuse me. I don't mean to tell
          you your business, but her heart
          was the only part of her that
          worked well.

                    CORONER
          Ain't working now.

Coroner finishes writing, hands David a slip.

                    CORONER
          Want my advice? Don't tell a soul
          she's dead. Stick her in a sack,
          take her down the service
          elevator, if there is one, and then
          sublease the apartment.

David has no chance to react before the coroner leaves. David watches,
shakes his head.

NOTE: The entire scene is correct.

CHAPTER
13

Writing Teleplays

So you want to write for television? For twenty-two episodes a year, can you create funny lines for:

1. Hit men?
2. Sewer maintenance operators?
3. NFL replay judges?
4. Waxed dental floss makers?

Do you think you can pen a one-hour lawyer-cop-social worker-action-adventure show that also includes a precocious but lovable teenager? If the answer to either question is yes, then TV may be perfect for you.

Most primetime offerings fall into three categories. These are Movies of the Week (MOW), one-hour shows, and the half-hour form—usually sitcom or dramedy. The teleplay format for MOWs and one-hour shows is similar to that of filmscripts. Format for half-hours, however, is substantially different from filmscripts. Let's look first at half-hour scripts.

The major format differences between half-hour teleplays and filmscripts are:

Slugs are <u>underlined</u>.
Directions are in all CAPS.

Dialogue is double-spaced.

There are scene and act breaks.

Parentheticals are used more freely.

The parenthetical continuing is shown differently.

The Scene letter is included with the page number.

Continueds are not used.

In half-hour format, a *scene break* occurs when there is a major change in location, time, and sometimes action. For viewers this scene-ending is usually signified by a dissolve from the present set to a exterior stock shot of the next set, or by an immediate shift to the next set. The writer indicates a scene break by ending one scene with a cut and beginning the next scene on the following page. Scenes are designated alphabetically, beginning with A, sometimes excluding the letter I.

An *act break* is a place in the script where the story reaches a climactic moment, one in which the audience is eager to discover what will happen next. At that point the drama pauses for the ultimate question of television: Can the commercial grab you before you grab the channel changer?

Acts are designated numerically. However, the act number is usually written out but sometimes shown in Roman numerals. The writer breaks an act by placing END OF ACT ONE, or END OF ACT I centered, in all caps, sometimes underlined, double-spaced beneath the cut or fade that ends the scene. The half-hour teleplay generally has one act break, that is, it contains two acts.

Begin most half-hour scripts by writing the name of the show, centered and capped, six lines from the top of the page. Double-space down from the name of the show, and write the title of the episode, in upper-and-lower case type, centered, and enclosed in quotation marks. Six lines beneath the title, cap, underline, and center <u>ACT ONE</u>. Then five lines below <u>ACT ONE</u>, write <u>A</u>, also capped, centered, and underlined.

Eight lines below <u>A</u>, you begin the actual teleplay by writing FADE IN: As in a filmscript, FADE IN: begins at 1.4 inches from the paper's left edge. The first slug is written two spaces below FADE IN:. The first page of a half-hour teleplay generally begins:

<u>NAME OF SHOW</u>

"Title of Episode "

<u>ACT ONE</u>

<u>A</u>

FADE IN:

<u>INT. COMMISSIONER'S OFFICE - DAY</u>

As mentioned above, half-hour teleplays end each *scene* on a CUT TO:, DISSOLVE TO:, FADE TO:, or other cut. To begin a new scene — say, scene <u>B</u> — you usually leave the top third of the page, except for the page number, blank. About 21 lines from the top of the page, write <u>B</u>, centered, capped, and underlined. Then, six lines beneath the scene's letter designation, write your opening slug. The first page of a new scene begins:

B

<u>INT. LIVING ROOM - DAY</u>

You generally begin an act by placing the act number (ACT TWO), centered, ten lines from the top edge of the page. Six lines beneath the act number, write the scene's letter designation, in caps, centered, and underlined. Six lines below the letter, place the term FADE IN:. Then double-space to your slug. If there is only one act break in your teleplay (as is the case for most sitcoms), make it as close to the script's midpoint as possible. On the last page of the teleplay, some shows use <u>THE END</u> instead of END OF ACT TWO. Most do not.

As you know, each page of a screenplay equals approximately one minute of screen time. This is not true for half-hour scripts. Because each scene in a half-hour teleplay begins on a new page and because the dialogue is double-spaced, a half-hour teleplay is approximately forty-four to forty-eight pages, equalling about a half-minute of TV time per page.

Placement of the page number is the same in both teleplays and filmscripts. However, in most teleplays the page number is followed by a period:

17.

In many half-hour teleplays, the scene's letter designation, enclosed in parentheses, appears single-spaced below the period that follows the page number or below the last number in the page number. In the opening page of the scene, there is no letter designation under the page number or the period. So if page 17 is in scene D, it is written:

17.
(D)

or

17.
(D)

The use of the parenthetical continuing is different in teleplays. In teleplays when a character's speech is interrupted, if his or her following dialogue continues with the rest of the speech, the continuation is noted by writing in parenthesis the abbreviated form (CONT'D) by the side of the character cue. This is shown:

```
                    AL
          This isn't the time to be...

                    ED
          ... taking risks.

                    AL (CONT'D)
          ... trying to guess what others
          will say.
```

The general rules above apply to almost every half-hour teleplay. Still, among the half-hour series there are a number of differences in script format. Some series enclose all direction in parenthesis. Some series that enclose direction in parenthesis eliminate the period at the end of the last sentence in the direction and use only the closing parenthesis mark.

At the beginning of each scene, most, but not all, half-hour teleplays list all the characters who will be in the scene. The characters' names usually appear in upper and lower-case type, single-spaced beneath the scene's opening slug, sometimes enclosed in parentheses:

```
INT. DRESSING ROOM - DAY
(Joe, Raccoon, Toby, Gertrude,
Ape-man, Bluster Belly, Godzilla)
```

Some half-hour shows leave the right-hand third of each page blank. This, I have been told, is so that the cast and crew can write changes and instructions in the wide right-hand margins.

What about the format for one-hour shows and MOWs? One-hour shows are formatted like filmscripts, except they include act breaks. You begin and end those act breaks as you do for a sitcom. Unlike a sitcom, however, hour shows do not include scene breaks. An hour teleplay contains between fifty and fifty-five pages, each page equivalent to approximately one minute of screen time.

What about the MOW? Is there a special format for it? Not really. An MOW resembles a filmscript, except that most MOW scripts have seven act breaks. However, even if you feel your filmscript will make a terrific TV movie, unless it is being written specifically for a TV movie, don't include act breaks. Format your filmscript as though it will be a theatrical release. If your agent sells your script to television, you can then make the necessary changes.

Bind a teleplay just as you would bind a filmscript. On the title page, however, write the name of the show, centered, capped, and underlined. Then double-space and write the title of the episode, in upper- and lower-case type, centered, and enclosed in quotation marks. Complete the rest of the title page as you would for a filmscript.

There are numerous shows on the air, and there will be many new ones by the time this book is published. Therefore, no single chapter could list every nuance of television script format. The best way to learn the format for *any* half-hour or one-hour show is to read some teleplays from that show. Read at least one, but preferably two or more, scripts from the show and copy the show's format exactly. If you can write good one-hour or funny half-hour teleplays, you may have a future in television.

Part Four

WITH
A LITTLE
HELP FROM
YOUR
FRIENDS

CHAPTER
14

Read My Tips

For most writers who submit scripts to Hollywood, the phrase, "does not meet our present needs" has a dreadful familiarity. Sure, it could mean they really liked your script but they are working on something similar. It could also mean they really liked your script but it isn't the type of screenplay they want now. It could mean those things, but generally it means, "We'll buy your script the day there is a cure for the common cold, peace in the Middle East, and the Cleveland Indians win the World Series."

Getting those first few rejection letters isn't too awful. Almost every writer has, at some time, received rejection letters. After a while, however—say, by the second week—disappointment sets in.

One way to overcome that disappointment is to rationalize that the phrase, "does not meet our present needs" is still better than, "you have the right to remain silent." A better approach is to seek some help for your script. That help might come from friends, an editor, and/or a writers' group.

Usually, the people we first ask to read our work are friends. But writers need to view friends' comments with perspective. Friends do not want to hurt your feelings. So no matter how much you assure them that the friendship will not suffer, friends may not be completely candid.

Putting friendship to such a stringent test can be nerve-wracking. Still, there are some important things you can learn from a friend's reading. And this is not a bad start toward getting at least some sense of how well your screenplay succeeds.

If you can watch a friend read some of your screenplay, your friend's body language will often give you significant signals about your story. Does your friend fidget as he or she reads? Do his eyes stay with the page or wander? Does she laugh at the comic parts? Does he turn the pages faster during action scenes? What is your friend's expression(s) as she reads? All these can indicate your friend's reaction to the material.

A friend's comments, even if general, can be helpful. If you hear a particular criticism only once or twice, you can probably chalk it up to someone's personal preference. However, if you receive the same criticism several times, it is best to at least think about a revision.

Whenever someone reads your work—before you send it to agents, producers, etc.—ask him or her to note any errors in spelling, punctuation, or grammar (S-P-G). Even after you and your computer software have worked it into what you believe is perfect shape, there can always remain that small typo, misspelling, or other error that was overlooked.

To assure yourself of excellent S-P-G, you may consider employing the services of a good editor. A good editor is a person who holds dear the English language and can correct your S-P-G problems. An editor might also point out where your writing is unclear or your story too vague.

Much of what an editor will do for your script depends on time and money—his or her time; your money. If you feel somewhat uncertain about your writing and you have the money, hiring an editor to help you—not only with S-P-G, but also with clarity—is not a bad idea.

However, be aware of the difference between a qualified editor and a fee reader. Fee readers are people who read and critique scripts for a flat fee—usually a substantial number of dollars. They often advertise themselves as agents, script doctors, or, sometimes, instructors.

While there may be one or two excellent and honest fee readers, most simply want your money. They are not necessarily qualified to critique your script, nor do they care about you or your script. They will keep reading as long as you keep seeding. So to save yourself time, money, and heartache, *avoid* those who read for a fee.

How do you find a good editor? Try asking friends, writers' organizations, and schools. You might also contact local print shops—as frequently editors work and/or advertise with them—as well as local publishers, and college English departments. An English graduate student may be perfect.

No editor can help a bad script sell. But even a terrific story will be rejected if the writing is unclear and the S-P-G is wretched. A good editor can help you improve your script. And that improvement can make a tremendous difference.

Another excellent way to improve your writing is to join a writers' group. Screenwriters, however, face particular problems that prose, poetry, and even playwrights do not encounter. Therefore, as a screenwriter, it is necessary to carefully assess whether a particular group is right for you.

The problem for screenwriters, as I am sure you know, stems from the unique nature of the screenplay. Almost any group of literate, attentive writers is familiar with prose, poetry, or plays, and probably can offer fine critique on original material. However, judging a screenplay for content and format requires specialized knowledge.

Most people who have not studied or written films do not have a good understanding of the requirements. In analyzing a script, they have only a rudimentary idea of what to judge. It would be akin to trying to referee a rugby game when you are familiar only with football. Quite simply, it will not work.

Even if you find a group that is knowledgeable, you need to decide whether it is the group for you. Groups, like people, have different personalities, and it might be important to your progress to choose the type of group from which you would best benefit.

I helped found one successful writing group—of non-screenwriters—that has been in existence for twelve years. This group takes a serious approach in its sessions. During its meetings, someone reads, the others carefully evaluate, another person reads, and so on.

While the publishing record of this group has been outstanding, some might find this type of group too serious and straightforward. Yes, you want a hard, honest assessment, but you may also like a slightly less disciplined atmosphere. On the other hand, some groups can go too far the other way.

Some groups, for instance, love movies but really would rather discuss and see them, enjoy themselves, and party. This is a fabulous pastime, one of my favorites. But while you and I might like this approach as much as the next guy (Groucho would say, "Then I'll talk to the next guy"), we may have to consider the time we (don't) have.

How do you find a screenwriters' group? The same way you find a good editor. Ask people if they know of a local filmwriters' group. Call the local college English, writing, or film departments or local newspaper. If your community has a theater or two that shows the so-called small and/or art films, ask there. If you cannot find a group, you might form one yourself. How?

Plan a meeting at a central public place that has plenty of good, safe parking. Try to get a press release in the newspaper and on the radio via public service announcements. Have flyers printed that can be posted in libraries, bookstores, video shops, etc., and phone everyone you know who might be interested.

If you get the publicity, the initial response will be large, probably larger than you could handle for regular meetings. However, do not worry. Many people are simply curious and will not stay with the group long. The serious ones will become the group's core, and they will continue to meet.

At the initial meeting, decide what night of the week you want to meet, how often, and where. Also decide on goals and guidelines.

Some suggested guidelines:

1. When critiquing, always acknowledge the good points in a script.
2. Ideas, scenes, plots, and stories are not to be discussed with anyone outside the group until the writer says his or her story can be made public.
3. Take time for sharing pertinent information or strategies for writing, selling, or working in the business.
4. Make copies of your work so that other group members can comment on your format and S-P-G as well as content.

Also, keep in mind that any person's success helps the group as a whole.

My Nashville screenwriting group grew out of my classes in screenwriting. As of this writing, one writer has sold two screenplays, and several others have either optioned their scripts or found representation by agents. Another writer became story editor and head writer for a syndicated sitcom, and others have won or placed in the top five in screenwriting contests sponsored by the Wisconsin Screenwriter's Forum, Houston International Film Festival, Writer's Digest, World Pater Awards, and Image Film/Video.

The success record of this group, in existence for only five years, is remarkable for a group of filmwriters outside Los Angeles or New York. Its members have helped each other succeed. And the right group may help you as well. A group can serve as friend and editor, and give a writer that extra boost that could make the difference between hope and actual success.

CHAPTER
15

Word Processing:
The Times They Are A-changin'

This chapter is for those of you who write your scripts with word processors or who are thinking seriously about purchasing a word processing (WP) program. You've heard that formatting a screenplay with WP is no problem so long as you also add one of those special scriptwriting programs. Unfortunately, those special scriptwriting programs can be expensive.

If you'd rather not spend megadollars to format your scripts, you have an alternative. The two most popular WP programs, Microsoft Word and WordPerfect, contain everything you need to write a script in correct format. While neither Microsoft Word nor WordPerfect comes with a built-in style sheet for filmscripts, both programs give you the means to create a style sheet that will correctly format your filmscripts as you type.

With a film format style sheet, you do not need to buy or to learn an expensive and complicated supplemental program. This saves both money and time.

If you use or plan to use Microsoft Word or WordPerfect and can write a style sheet for formatting a filmscript, you should do so. If you cannot or do not want to spend the time it could take, then you might consider buying an inexpensive, already prepared style sheet. With a film format style sheet, by typing just one extra key you can:

1. center and cap your title six lines from the top of the page.
2. triple-space and begin your slug in all caps from horizontal space fourteen.

3. double-space to horizontal space fourteen and write direction in regular prose paragraph form.

5. double-space to horizontal space forty-one and cap the character cue as you write it.

6. single-space to horizontal space thirty-five for the occasional parenthetical.

7. after the character cue, single space to horizontal space twenty-eight while automatically adjusting the right and left margins for speech.

8. single-space within direction or dialogue.

9. double-space between direction paragraphs, direction and dialogue, dialogue and dialogue, dialogue and direction, direction and a cut, or dialogue and a cut.

10. double-space to horizontal space sixty-one and place cuts and FADE OUT: in caps.

With a few other simple and easy to learn "tricks," Microsoft Word or WordPerfect will:

1. move the cursor to horizontal space forty-one, write the character cue in caps, and then single-space to horizontal space twenty-eight, where you can begin typing the speech.

2. triple-space to horizontal space fourteen, write out your slug in caps, and then double-space to horizontal space fourteen, where you can begin typing directions.

3. allow you to format on the screen as you type the script—unlike many of the script programs.

4. never leave a slug or character cue as the last item on a page. (Properly set, the program must have either direction or dialogue following a slug and dialogue following a character cue or the slug or cue will be automatically moved to the next page.)

5. never begin a page with a CUT TO: or MATCH CUT:

6. never break up a paragraph of direction or dialogue and move part of it to a new page. (Writers who find this a problem may easily eliminate this feature from the sheet.)

7. automatically paginate and repaginate.

I offer both Microsoft Word and WordPerfect scriptwriting style sheets for IBM compatible machines. The style sheet program is available on either a 5¼- or 3½-inch disk. An instruction brochure accompanies the disk. If you want to order the program, write to:

> Film Style
> Reichman Enterprises
> PO Box 2592
> Merrifield, VA 22116-2592

and enclose a check or money order for $75.00. I and some of my students have been using these programs for years, and they work well.

CHAPTER
16

Finale

Is there a chance, really, for someone outside the film industry to actually sell a screenplay or teleplay? Again and again, I hear from agents and producers that Hollywood is always seeking talented new writers. Warner Brothers Television holds workshops, not only in Los Angeles but also in other areas of the country, in order to find new writers for their sitcoms. Every year new writers do sell scripts. Some even win Academy Awards.

"Okay, so Hollywood is buying from some new writers," you think. "But honestly, doesn't the industry already know what it wants? Aren't they mostly purchasing the same old action-adventure, "buns and guns" formula screenplays that are now being written by a bunch of kids who either have great contacts and/or went to film school?" Not necessarily.

Most of the time, "the industry" has no idea what it wants or from whom it wants it. William Goldman, in his marvelous book *Adventures in the Screen Trade,* wrote, "Nobody knows nothing." Nobody knows what will sell or won't sell in the future. What is popular today probably will not be popular tomorrow. What is rejected one day is often the smash hit of the day after.

Whatever the odds against success, there are writers who beat those odds. And it is not always the most talented writers who succeed. As my father often reminded me, to be successful in any worthwhile endeavor, "It ain't the IQ but the I DO that counts."

Now that you know how to put a screenplay on paper, you may want to know more about structure, characterization, and how to market your screenplay. There are a number of good books on those topics. I have included a list of my favorites—and the books that my students favor—at the end of this book.

I hope this book has been helpful and that you will recommend it—preferably not the copy you have!—to others.

Index of Important Terms

ACT BREAK: Where a teleplay breaks for a commercial (page 158).

AD LIB: General extemporaneous chatter among a group of people (page 81).

AMPERSAND (&): A symbol for the word "and," placed between authors' names on the title page to indicate that they are partners in the authorship of the script (page 139).

AND: Used between authors' names on the title page to indicate that the author whose name appears first wrote the script, and the author whose name appears after "and" rewrote it (page 139).

AUTHOR'S SCRIPT: What you, the author, write; does not contain "production script" details (page xiii-xiv).

B.G.: Background (page 83).

BACK TO SCENE: Returns the reader to the shot before the previous slug (page 41).

CHARACTER CUE: In dialogue, the name of the character who speaks the subsequent line(s) (page 53-54).

CHARACTER'S SPEECH: What the character says in dialogue (page 53-54).

CUT TO: Tells the reader that a shot, scene, or sequence of the script is finished and a new one will follow (page 98-100).

DIALOGUE: The speech of a screenplay (page 53).

DIRECTION: That part of the script that delineates the action and describes characters, settings, and objects. It is the means by which the writer indicates the visual images he or she wants on the screen (page 25).

"DOES NOT MEET OUR PRESENT NEEDS": A literary phrase that, loosely translated, means, "Do not quit your day job" (page 167).

DRAMEDY: A film or TV show with an almost even mix of drama and comedy (page 157).

EXT.: Exterior (page 12).

EXT./INT, or INT./EXT.: Used when you need to show two adjoining sets—one outside and one inside—simultaneously (page 44).

F.G.: Foreground (page 83).

FADE IN: Begins your screenplay (page 97-98).

FADE OUT: Ends your screenplay (page 97-98).

FEE READERS: People who read and critique scripts for a fee—usually a substantial one (page 168).

FILLERS (IN SPEECH): Meaningless words or phrases that are peppered into naturalistic speech (page 70).

FLAG PAGE: A screenplay page that alternates a line or two of direction and a line or two of dialogue all the way down the page (page 145).

INT.: Interior (page 12).

INTERCUT: A rapid cutting between two or more people and locations; conveys the idea that the actions are happening more or less simultaneously (page 43-44).

MARGINALS: The small but significant items found at the margins of the page. These items include the title, continueds, page numbers, and <u>THE END</u> (page 109).

MARKETING: The means of selling your screenplay (page 174).

MATCH CUT: The use of a physical object to bridge shots, scenes, or sequences (page 100-102).

MONTAGE: Two or more images that blend into and out of each other in order to create a particular emotional effect (page 40).

MOS: A German term meaning without sound (page 81).

MOW: Movie of the Week (page 157; also see 163).

NATURALISM: Trying to perfectly imitate real life (page 70).

O.S.: Off screen; signifies that the character speaking or the cause of a particular noise, though nearby, is not shown in the scene (page 83-84).

PARENTHETICAL: Personal direction; refers to instructions to the actors enclosed in parentheses and placed directly beneath the character cue or sometimes within the speech (page 54-55).

POV: Point of view; indicates that the audience sees literally through the eyes of *one* character. In film, POV is a straight-ahead shot, without peripheral vision (page 42-43).

PRESENT: Refers to when the screenplay is shot rather than when the screenplay is written (page 14).

PRIMARY SLUG: The slug that introduces a scene and gives three pieces of information: EXT. or INT.; place; and time of day (page 12).

PRODUCTION SCRIPT: Script that contains camera angles, scene numbers, directive parentheticals, and various other technical information, which help in budgeting and shooting the film (page xiii-xiv).

PUBLIC DOMAIN: Status of an artistic work which was never copyrighted or for which the copyright has expired (page 82).

READER OR COVERAGE EDITOR: A person who reads and reports on scripts (this task is called coverage) that a studio or agency is considering (page xiii).

REDUNDANT PREPOSITIONS: Prepositions that repeat the meaning of the previous word, i.e. "continued on" (page 70).

SCENE: A section of the script (generally three-and-a-half to seven pages or minutes—one page equals one minute of screen time) possessing a definitive beginning, middle, and end and centering on a theme and/or action. Usually, it is comprised of a sequence of shots that move the scene to its conclusion (page 12).

SCENE BREAK: A TV term signifying a major change in location, time, and sometimes action. This scene-ending is usually indicated for viewers by a dissolve from the present set to a exterior stock shot of the next set or by an immediate shift to the next set (page 158).

SECONDARY SLUG: The first and only slug that heads a shot (page 15-16).

SEQUENCE: Consecutive scenes that center on a theme and/or action and, like a scene, contain a beginning, middle, and end (page 100).

SERIES OF SHOTS: A group of short shots that move a character quickly through a period of time (page 39-40).

SFX: Sound effects (page 41-42).

SHOT: A part of the script that includes the slug and all content until the next slug (page 11-12).

SITCOM: Situation comedy (page 11; also see 154-158).

SLUG LINES: The always-capped, single-line entries that begin a scene or shot (page 11).

SPFX: Special effects (page 41-42).

SPLIT SCREEN: A device for showing events and people in different locations simultaneously on screen (page 44).

STOCK SHOT: A shot, usually exterior, used repeatedly in a TV series (page 158).

STRUCTURE: The formula for writing a screenplay (page 174).

TALKING HEADS: Scenes in a filmscript where two or more characters talk endlessly (page 69).

T PAGE: A screenplay page that begins or ends with a directional paragraph, but fills the rest of the page with dialogue. This pattern forms a large T, either right-side up or inverted, on the page (page 147).

TELEPLAY: A script for a TV show, usually for a half-hour sitcom (page 157).

TITLE PAGE: The first page in your script. The page on which you place the *title*, the name(s) of the *author(s)*, *company name* if applicable, *address*, and *phone number*, and sometimes other information about the script (page 137).

V.O.: Voice over; is used when a character who cannot be in the shot speaks; to transmit a character's voice over an electronic medium such as a telephone or television; or for narration, whether the character speaking is on screen or not (page 83-85).

WIDER VIEW: A term meaning the enlargement of the area initially seen around a person or object (page 40-41).

Suggested Reading

Alley, Robert, & Irby Brown. *Murphy Brown: Anatomy of a Sitcom.* New York: Dell, 1990.

Aristotle. *Poetics.*

Bach, Steven. *Final Cut.* New York: William Morrow, 1985.

Brady, John. *The Craft of the Screenwriter.* New York: Simon and Schuster, 1981.

Egri, Lajos. *The Art of Dramatic Writing.* New York: Simon and Schuster, 1960.

Field, Syd. *Screenplay.* New York: Dell Publishing, 1984.

————. *Selling a Screenplay: The Screenwriter's Guide to Hollywood.* New York: Dell Publishing, 1989.

Gitlin, Todd. *Inside Prime Time.* New York: Pantheon, 1983.

Goldman, William. *Adventures in the Screentrade.* New York: Warner Books, 1983. (I recommend the paperback version because it contains a copy of the screenplay *Butch Cassidy and the Sundance Kid.*)

Kosberg, Robert, with Mim Eichler. *How to Sell Your Idea to Hollywood.* New York: Harper Perennial, 1991.

Litwak, Mark. *Reel Power.* New York: William Morrow, 1986.

Packard, William. *The Art of Screen-Writing.* New York: Paragon House, 1987.

Sayles, John. *Thinking in Pictures.* Boston: Houghton Mifflin, 1987.

Seger, Linda. *Making a Good Script Great.* New York: Samuel French Trade, 1987.

Walter, Richard. *Screenwriting.* New York: Plume/New American Library, 1988.

Whitcomb, Cynthia. *Selling Your Screenplay.* New York: Crown, 1988.

And all the screenplays and teleplays you can find.

About the Author

RICK Reichman graduated from the University of Southern California with an MFA in professional writing, emphasis in film writing. He has taught screenwriting classes in Nashville, Tennessee, and Washington, D.C. In 1990 he was one of 16 chosen—out of over 450 entries—for the Warner Brothers Sitcom Workshop in Baltimore. He has also been a finalist in the Wisconsin Screenwriter's Forum Screenwriting contest.

Reichman's students have done well. Some have sold and optioned their scripts. One student became head writer and story editor for a syndicated sitcom. Another won a prestigious Nicholl Fellowship, awarded by the Academy of Motion Picture Arts and Sciences and one other student won a Walt Disney Fellowship in screenwriting. Reichman's students have also won or placed in the top five in other screenwriting contests, including those sponsored by the Houston International Film Festival, Wisconsin Screenwriter's Forum, Image Film/Video of Atlanta, the Virginia Governor's competition, *Writers Digest,* and the World Pater Awards.

Reichman currently teaches at Georgetown University and at American University in Washington, D.C. He also conducts workshops and seminars in screenwriting. Presently, Reichman is finishing several screenplays and teleplays.